academic
POLITICS

academic
POLITICS

William R. Brown

The University of Alabama Press
University, Alabama

Library of Congress Cataloging in Publication Data

Brown, William R.
  Academic politics.

  Bibliography: p.
  Includes index.
  1. Universities and colleges—United States—
Administration. 2. Politics and education—United States. 3. Universities and col-
leges—United States
—Faculty. I. Title.
LB2341.B68   378.73   81-23100
ISBN 0-8173-0116-X   AACR2

For
Loje

CONTENTS

Preface   ix

1. The Problem of the Academy   1

2. The Dependent Entrepreneur:
   Individual Performance in Academia   17

3. Organization without Structure:
   The Academic Department   40

4. Equations of Power:
   The Academician and the University   65

5. The Academic Political Paradigm   102

6. Faculty Unions and the Academic Perception   127

Notes   173

Bibliography   180

Index   184

PREFACE

The experience that is most likely to stimulate the imagination is an encounter with an unusual aspect of something we otherwise accept and see as being familiar. New questions arise because an object, idea, or individual that was supposedly understood proves mystifying. Such was my introduction to academic politics. As a political scientist, I had every reason to assume that explaining the internal politics of a university would simply be a matter of definition and analysis—sorting phenomena into one or another of the several categories used within the discipline for this purpose. Having worked for nearly twenty years in the federal bureaucracy, I also had experienced the intricacies of how institutions determine priorities, accepting one idea and favoring its proponents while ignoring the pleas of those who do not seem to relate so well to the demands of the moment. But from my experience as a political officer at American embassies in several Middle Eastern and Asian countries, I had learned that a single set of political perceptions could not explain politics under all conditions. Different cultures have different ways of expressing themselves.

To rely upon the well-worn concepts of the American polity is sometimes to take the easy way out. One such episode was my work in the political section of the embassy in Djakarta during the days of Sukarno. We busied ourselves reporting to the State Department in ways that depicted Sukarno as a charismatic but rational authoritarian leader. We worked within the interplay of power among the army, the veterans, the Muslim leaders, the communist party, and Sukarno—much as if Indonesia's struggles were taking place on the American scene. Actually they were taking place only in our American minds. Washington was satisifed. Some of our analysis may have appeared brilliant. In fact, it had little to do with the political scene we were observing.

My first insight into Javanese reality occurred one day when an Indonesian friend sensed that I was troubled and suggested that perhaps I could overcome my problems if I borrowed his magic kris. He immediately withdrew the offer, embarrassed by the lapse that had led him to forget our cultural differences. His excuse was that as a foreigner, I probably could not control a kris. It was too powerful, its use being familiar only to Javanese. But our relationship was close, and he eventually asked if I believed in the power of a kris. I told him that in my country I didn't believe, but that in his I couldn't dare to disbelieve. This single remark opened a whole new political world to me.

Our analysis in the American embassy was indeed deficient. As it turned out, Sukarno was intent upon collecting at his palace in Bogar the jewels owned by the sultan of Djogjarkarta. The sultan was believed by the people to be a descendant of the Goddess of the South Seas, and these gems possessed power. By purchase, stealth, trickery—whatever—Sukarno proceeded. In this way he hoped to increase his power and assure both political authority and personal vitality. It is no exaggeration to suggest that Sukarno fancied himself as Arjuna battling in the cosmos against the forces of evil.

At the same time, Indonesia's president employed a British adviser and speech writer who was supposedly a communist. Here was the essence of Western rationality. When Sukarno visited the United States in May 1956 this individual wrote into the president's speeches beautiful allusions to the political philosophy of Thomas Jefferson. The American ambassador was enthralled. The secretary of state concluded that we had enough in common with Sukarno to work with him. Sukarno's seeming familiarity with our political tradition made the reports of the embassy's political officers plausible. I never bothered to tell colleagues about the incident of the kris or to report to Washington on the sultan's jewels.

My introduction to academic politics was no different. Well along in mid-career I had entered a new culture, and I was perplexed by its politics. My initial response to faculty senates was reminiscent of Kipling's Mowgli upon his capture by the Bandar-log. There were indeed occasions when faculty seemed to gather by the hundreds to listen to speakers singing the praises of the group. And whenever a speaker stopped for want of breath, I could almost hear the group shout together: "This is true, we all say so." Like Mowgli, at some of the late night meetings I sometimes concluded that Tabaqui, the jackal, must have bitten all these people and now they had the madness. Did they never sleep?

During relaxed morning moments, I realized that there was some method—some system—behind the antics I had witnessed the evening before. It was just that the activity was being played out against a backdrop that did not seem to apply—a council employing parliamentary procedures based on the assumption that material interests were being served and constituencies were being represented within a deliberative process in which a division based on one person/one vote supposedly determined outcome. There was clearly incongruence between the events I was witnessing and the explanations of academic politics that relied on conventional concepts and patterns borrowed from pluralistic democracy or bureaucratic practice. I soon found that I was nurturing a well-developed preoccupation: how to explain academic politics in a way other than that which had heretofore been used to depict it.

This book is the result of my efforts. Along the way many people have contributed. Initially, Seymour Martin Lipset helped me give it order, and Allen Lacy attested to its veracity. Frank Wallin, Tom Bartlett, John Morris, and John Rexine contributed more than they know or are likely to admit. Faculty at Colgate University, Stockton State College, and Central Connecticut State College have all made their contributions through our daily exchanges—just in conducting the business of education. To all I am grateful for the access I have been allowed in my adopted profession. In the editing and reediting, Loje has been my critic. Janice Shockley, Gail Gregson, Helen Schlemp, Judy Filipek, and, most of all, Maureen Duly have helped me prepare several versions of the ideas presented here. I owe a lot—these are fine people.

Canton, Connecticut William R. Brown
November 1981

academic
POLITICS

1

The Problem of the Academy

What is the character of a university? Even asking the question portends uncertainty, and those to whom it is directed are often annoyed by being asked. Many consider the discussion of such a definition unseemly. If a university is meant to represent diversity, as many people believe, it will have different meanings for different people. The central character of a university or an individual's own university is usually accepted implicitly and not thought to need definition. More feeling than dispassion is associated with any description. The very term *alma mater* nurtures this sentiment. A university tends to fall into the same category as religion, patriotism, and kinship: we seldom puzzle over it; we know what it means. Yet, scholars and academicians have been pursuing the meaning of the modern university for the one hundred thirty years since John Henry Newman lectured on the subject at the Catholic University in Dublin.

In the stream of pragmatic American thought, the university is likely to be seen in terms of the process that takes place within it—teaching, learning, and, occasionally, thinking. It may also be seen as a distinct sector that produces either trained manpower or, in the case of applied research, answers to the social, scientific, and economic questions of our time. The more erudite will suggest that the university sustains our intellectual life, although other institutions and even individuals working outside an institutional context make major contributions to this activity as well.

Each of these definitions reflects, of course, an external perspective. None touches upon the internal workings of the university—its nature, spirit, or style. How many who have experience with a university understand the viewpoint of the academician—the producer of the university, so to speak, who remains in it and sees it as his place of toil?

When the academician maintains that the faculty is the university, what are the implications of this assertion? Need it be accepted by other constituencies—alumni, students, administrators, boards of trustees, or the general public?

By this time, no doubt, the annoyance that was suggested by the very consideration of this topic has begun to set in. Is there any reason for raising this question at all, or is it just to allow for an intellectual exercise on a matter that may fascinate the author but be of little concern beyond the narrow confines in which he works? Actually, the question has broad ramifications and practical consequences for the way higher education operates and what it will produce during the next decade.

The Setting

In the past thirty years, higher education has on at least two occasions successfully met the necessity for change. During the 1950s and until the mid-1960s, the situation called for growth. To the extent that changes in programs were involved, they expressed the need for new knowledge—an extension of science and scientific method to everything. Our colleges and universities adapted themselves admirably to this requirement. Then in the late 1960s and early 1970s, society fell into the grip of a curious turmoil generated by our youth. Pressures were for humanizing education, what some critics of our social scene considered to be a crude form of neoromanticism that gave heightened importance to the individual. Direct human experience became necessary in all aspects of life, even—or especially—in the classroom. Concern was for broadening the learning environment to allow for wider options in personal development, a more socially oriented curriculum, and freedom from the traditional structures associated with higher education. None of these themes was new. But after the mid-1960s they were intensified and accompanied by the excesses of sensationalism which in many cases replaced rationalism in the syllabuses of college courses. Nevertheless, higher education responded to the temper of the times.

These experiences suggest that a certain tension may perpetually exist between the demands of society and the academic establishment of colleges and universities. If a lesson can be drawn from the twenty-five years during which first scientism and then experientialism pervaded our educational experience, it is that academia does not mold society. In fact, higher education usually takes its lead from forces that are abroad in the land.

For the decade of the 1980s, yet another set of circumstances will provide the basis for a new tension between the academy and the society it serves. During a time of institutional growth, questions are seldom asked about the efficient use of resources. Trade-offs, priorities, and opportunity costs need not be considered too carefully. With the sense of opulence that existed in higher education during the 1950s and 1960s, it sometimes seemed as if anything could be done—almost at will. Nothing need wait its turn. But now, and probably for the remainder of the decade, a different mood prevails.

In recent years, higher education has attracted increased attention from centers of public authority in our society. State systems of higher education have emerged which impose heavy administrative overlays on publicly financed colleges and universities. The federal government has established one office after another in its efforts to administer the programs of financial support which it provides for students and for the colleges or universities that they attend. These developments could have been predicted. Total institutional income for higher education in the United States reached $56.7 billion annually in 1979/80 and was expected to climb to $71 billion in 1981/82. A fair portion of this amount comes from state legislatures, community councils, and the federal government. Federal grants, contracts, and appropriations for higher education in 1979/80 were over $7.75 billion. The funds made available through the National Science Foundation for research at universities approached $1 billion. State legislatures appropriated about $20 billion.[1] When public resources are committed to an endeavor or enterprise on such a grand scale, the politician cannot be far behind.

The tendency has been for government at all levels to attempt to impose controls over higher education in a way that public officials hope will clarify the goals of the colleges and universities under their jurisdiction. They want to limit unnecessary duplication and ascertain that the activities of these institutions conform to views of the citizenry with regard to what higher education as supported by taxation should be. In the case of both the scientific expansion of the 1950s and the humanizing of the curriculum during the mid-1960s and the early 1970s, the impulse for change came from society. But the ideas that were involved came from the universities themselves. Society pointed the way and the academicians picked it up from there. Now, as we look toward the future, we cannot identify the concepts of change with the academy. Outwardly, they take the form of a mania for efficiency. Actually, they are an effort to establish political control over one of the few partially free institutions remaining in our society.

Higher education is, of course, divided into public and private sectors. Some of those who are concerned with its future may conclude that whatever the machinations of bureaucrats, the well-being and the preservation of the independent intellect that finds protection in our centers of learning can be assured by private colleges and universities. More than one-third of all expenditures for higher education occur at private institutions. But even private colleges are influenced by the temper of the times and readily refashion their programs when such action is necessary to attract students and funds. Federally supported research and student grants at private schools, along with the influence that accompanies such beneficence, have brought almost every institution of higher education under a substantial degree of governmental influence. Some of our more prestigious universities have been converted into virtual "federal grant" institutions. As far back as the late 1960s no less a university than Stanford received 65 percent of its annual income from the federal government. In 1980, Princeton looked to federal grants for 41 percent of its budget, and the University of Miami received $60 million.[2] State governments also allocate public funds for private education.[3] In New York in 1978, $91 million in direct financial aid went to independent colleges. Pennsylvania used $38 million in public monies for this purpose, while other states allocated somewhat less.[4] Any college where students benefit from federal grants (which is just about every place of postsecondary education in the country) must abide by federal regulations.

One feature of the educational scene at the beginning of the 1980s that preplexed observers was the wide gap between the general sense of hard times or decline on most campuses and the actual reports on the financial condition of higher education. For 1980/81, the spending levels of states increased by 10 percent, being 18 percent above 1978/79 budgets. Federal outlays for higher education, including the budgets of the Departments of Education and Health and Human Resources, combined with veterans benefits and funds from the National Science Foundation, amounted to $13 billion. Enrollments for 1981/82 showed a slight increase. The number of colleges continued to grow, although most growth was by two-year institutions. One of the principal complaints—government interference—showed signs of abating as federal

officials promised relief from government rules and reporting requirements. But there was reason for apprehension. Student loans were to
be reduced, which raised fears over sustaining enrollments. The de-
mographic profile in some parts of the country pointed to fewer
students before the end of the decade, and this condition would bring
the probability of less support for the educational establishment. In
addition, allocations for the National Endowments for the Arts and
Humanities had been reduced substantially, and gifts from independent foundations had declined by 50 percent over the previous four
years. The Reagan administration promised less regulatory interference, but it also warned of less financial support for 1982 and
beyond.[5]

Various other factors also contributed to the depressed mood
among educators. The harbingers of smaller budgets were bad
enough, but of greater concern was the threat to the general liberal
interpretation of society which the occupants of most of our campuses
propound. That liberalism had been pummelled by the political success of conservatism. Many professional dispensers of "good and justice" through liberal causes had a difficult time comprehending the
circumstances that had led to Ronald Reagan's success at the polls. It
did not fit with their vision of the future. In addition, state governments
gave no sign that they would interfere less in the affairs of colleges and
universities, even though they talked of fewer dollars for higher education. Apportioning scarcity is itself a political matter, and politicians
were likely to demand a greater role in academic decision making. In
many respects, the future seemed certain. Unlike the 1950s and 1960s,
commissions, regents, and oversight bodies were now in place; legislators had an eye on education; and everyone was looking for something
to do. As a prelude to the future, it was only necessary to note that over
the past few years, colleges, their faculties, and boards of trustees had
initiated suits that reached the supreme courts of no fewer than five
states. The issue was always the same—efforts by legislatures to interfere unduly in the affairs of state universities.

Even on the national scene there was reason to doubt that higher
education would long be relieved of administrative interference. The
political agenda might change from one Washington administration to
the next, but the location of the country's brain power remains the
same—it is in our universities. Any new order in Washington might
only mean a shift in demands upon the university, from concern for
social programs, for example, to requests that attention be focused on

defense. In this regard, the question for the educational establishment at the beginning of the 1980s was not necessarily whether deliverance from federal regulations was worth the loss of government largesse. More than likely, the issue would be whether federal authority would bring a heavier hand than in the 1950s, the last time higher education was called upon to turn its attention to military matters. And academia may not respond in innocence as it did the last time. It may question the appropriateness of Washington's requests. Could defense-related demands and academia's response be yet the fourth occasion in our lifetime for a new expression of the perpetual tension that seems to exist between the academy and society?

The Academician's Concern

There are those who believe that losses in the quality of education occur whenever outside directors bring alien concepts of management to our institutions of higher learning. Certainly, many academicians contend, the result is substantial sacrifice in the independence that sparks scientific, social, and artistic inquiry. Academicians maintain that this loss could be of long duration and debilitating for our culture as a whole. But some outsiders consider this claim intangible and at worst a flimsy pretext for academic fecklessness. After measuring the antics of individual professors as sanctioned by academic freedom against the political here and now of billions of dollars in public allocations for higher education, many observers would conclude that a drive for efficiency in our colleges and universities has come none too soon. Yet, our system of higher education has traditionally rested upon the entrepreneurial spirit of the individual academician—the very academician who is often accused of perpetuating the excesses that many political figures now believe must be eliminated from public higher education in the name of greater accountability and a more responsive attitude toward the dynamics of our society.

The issue as seen by the Chicago sociologist, Edward Shils, is whether the government's financial indulgence of universities gives it the right to regard them as instruments of its social, economic, and military policy and to interfere in the educational and intellectual process which, if distorted, reduces the quality of teaching and re-search.[6] J. M. Cameron of the University of Toronto has observed that education is a powerful instrument for the interpretation of life. There is a growing assumption, he fears, "that it is the business of the State, having under its hand the potent engine of education, to present us with a satisfactory plan to action....To entertain such expectations of the State and of its bureaucratic instruments is dangerous;...it may breed delusions of grandeur of statesmen who may conceive vast and vain ambitions....Restructuring a university is necessarily a painful process; it checks precisely those energies that are needed for the reconstruction of the university *as* a university."[7] The assumption underlying Shils's and Cameron's arguments is that the business of the university and the conditions under which this business is conducted are areas into which neither the public nor its civil servants has developed much insight.

A Proposition

But the various branches and levels of government are not swayed by this argument. The question, then, is whether a means can be found for adapting the techniques of management and planning to an institution that was fashioned to allow the practitioners of the academic arts maximum freedom in pursuing individual intellectual interests. Certainly, society, by providing resources, has the authority to dictate whatever changes it wants. But tightening administration and still preserving an atmosphere that enhances knowledge will not be possible unless there is a better understanding by government and the public of how a college or university operates. If we are to evade the risks of inadvertently converting some of our colleges into training centers that impart facts and perhaps skills but engender no intellectual speculation and growth, if we are to avoid the urge for professionalism at the undergraduate level that impels students to rush headlong toward one career or another without paying attention to people or ideas, then aspiring managers must develop an appreciation of the intricacies of the institutions they would direct—institutions that traditionally have operated for their own sake.

Politics is a means by which all groups in our society protect whatever they may consider dear. An important key to developing an appropriate appreciation of our colleges and universities, therefore, may be an understanding of the academician's politics. In the face of the threats posed by outside interference, academic politics—a matter that is often the subject of ridicule even among academicians themselves—becomes pertinent. The proposition set forth in this book is that the manner in which academicians organize themselves and the institutional relationships through which they create a college's internal politics are inherent to higher education as we know it today. By changing the university in order to achieve greater efficiency in the use of resources, the politicians and their managers might not detract from the training potential of any institution. But such a change, with the control it would imply, could bring a serious decline in the energy of the free-floating intellect—the individual ingenuity in matters of the mind that is an intangible but critical part of any national heritage. This book is intended to give university administrators, as well as the outside managers from the commissioners' offices and the state houses, a better understanding of an institution with which they might be tempted to tamper.

Despite contrasts that will be drawn between the academician working within our colleges and the manager representing our pluralistic society, my message is not that their viewpoints are irreconcilable. Rather, it is that good university management over the next decade will consist of working simultaneously within the framework of two perceptions. The totality of administrative practice cannot be premised simply on a set of universal rules directed toward achieving the abstractions involved in something called "efficiency." Management is, after all, a human endeavor, and when unusual organizing principles are encountered, as they are in academia, there may be virtue in assuming that the academicians who observe these principles have reasons—and usually good reasons—for behaving as they do.

The value of this book may become most apparent when tensions within a university are running high and contention surrounds much of what an administrator hopes to achieve. At that time, it can provide a point of view, a positive means of thinking about the political purposes of the academician. Several prescriptions for administrators operating within a university are implied by the academician's values as presented in these pages. The principles have not been reduced to a list of rules for administrative conduct. Variations in institutional circumstance and personal style will require individual managers to apply them differently. But the distinct guidelines which administrators may derive from this characterization of a university can have a common element—the need to cultivate a higher level of sensitivity toward the attitudes of the academicians with whom the managers work. The good manager knows his organization.

Any success in simultaneously applying both the norms of the academician and the practices that drive our open society will require a recognition on the part of the manager that those practices which he cloaks in the garb of utility often do not lead to a more efficient use of resources or even to the formulation and fulfillment of institutional objectives that better serve the public's needs or correspond to its demands. Rather, the administrator's objectives are often an effort on the part of management to increase its own influence at the expense of the traditional independence of the academician. Bureaucratic practice and aims are an old story in our society. In this one instance, there is surely merit in not deceiving ourselves by pretending that many of the actions initiated under management's direction accomplish anything other than an aggrandizement of the managers' prerogatives.

A View of Academia

Whenever we encounter the unfamiliar, we usually attempt to understand it by likening our sensation to something we have experienced before. The genius of human intelligence, in fact, is in the ability to make such contrasts and comparisons—to categorize phenomena. Herein lies the basis for the most useful concept of intellectual expression—the generalization. From it we develop abstractions. With the invention of the computer we have even found a way of getting a machine to make comparisons for us. But if the similarities we think we see in two situations are superficial in their nature, and if we miss the profound meaning of the unfamiliar condition, then to the extent that we act upon our conclusions, we risk making changes in our environment and society that are less beneficial than if we had seen things differently. The alternatives, the "might have beens" of history, go undetected.

And so it is with our universities and colleges. We can perceive features in their structure and operation that are similar to those of other organizations. In certain ways universities at least outwardly resemble a large bureaucracy consisting of a president, vice-presidents, deans, department chairmen, and faculty, all with supporting staff and all seeming to work in a hierarchy. Bureaucratic subdivisions devoted to student, administrative, academic, and public affairs are readily apparent. We assume, therefore, that orders are sent down through the structure, that subordinates respond, and that the work of the university is performed. From this viewpoint, institutional relationships within a college or university would quite naturally develop along the same lines as in a public or corporate bureaucracy.

The key to understanding a bureaucracy from a description of its structural features is the element of command and response according to detailed regulations that prescribe the actions of individuals working within the organization. In a well-run bureaucracy, behavior can be predicted simply by consulting rules, regulations, and job descriptions. These provide the focus for all activity. They offer an organizing theme. Performance is assessed from the standpoint of efficiency—how well does the employee keep the agency operating consistent with the expectations of its regulations?

Another aspect of institutional behavior is illustrated by the example of industry. In the name of standardization and cost-effectiveness, all functions have been simplified so that the individual can adapt his working patterns to a machine, which usually achieves only one step in a process. The final product results from a tight interdependence among individuals, while their machines perform different but related functions at the same time and pace. Performance is assessed in terms of productivity—the capability of the worker to assure that no delays or problems of quality occur in production. Perhaps the most pervasive feature of modern industrial society has been the interdependence associated with social and economic constraints. Caught in the web of impersonal relationships, disciplined by the division of labor, and exposed to the mass communications of modern differentiated life, the individual has lost the personal association with those aspects of his livelihood which characterized existence before the industrial revolution. Production is destined for exchange rather than direct consumption; the individual may be engaged in producing a component for which he does not understand the final purpose, much less use in his daily life. The very core of his livelihood can have little meaning other than the sustenance it provides. In modern society, participation is total insofar as most individuals must produce in some interrelated fashion in order for all to survive. Along with this interdependence has come a well-defined social structure.

None of these situations describes working conditions in our colleges. Few such solitary professions remain in our society today as that of the academician. Although he may reside in a large university and spend most of his time talking with or at others, the academician generally works alone. He prepares his own material, conducts his own courses, and evaluates his own students. The same singularity is present in much of his research. In this sense, academic performance is discrete. The academician is independent. The interdependence and division of labor that dominate relationships in a bureaucratic or industrial structure are not strong forces in academia. An understanding of academic politics begins with recognition of this distinction.

Working alone has one overriding result for an academician's activities. It means that no matter what he produces, his daily routine need not mesh with that of colleagues. His performance is holistic. The product is solely his. Consequently, he can have a sense of creativity. Pretensions of creativity are a strong current underlying academic life.

All people who work face the issues of legitimacy in what they do and integrity in how they do it. Bureaucrats gain legitimacy by identifying with the agency of employment. Integrity is found in working effectively toward the institution's goals according to the institution's rules. In industry, speed, dexterity, and low rejection rates for the items produced provide the measure of authenticity. It is called workmanship. For those who follow artistic pursuits, legitimacy can be provided by critics' acclaim as in the case of a noted painter or actor. There was even a time when various roles performed in society were said to be sanctioned by God.

But for the academician, rectitude has a different basis. Legitimacy is determined ascriptively. His position depends on an advanced degree—a Ph.D. in some area of intellectual or artistic concern. He may have a generalized commitment to a college and a demonstrated skill in teaching, but it is work within his discipline—his dedication and his contributions to a prescribed body of knowledge—that attests to his integrity. The academician's degree entitles him to undertake all sorts of activities in the name of creativity, even activities that on the surface, or at the moment, may offer no discernible value to mankind. Because of the degree, outsiders are supposed to assume that in his field of study, the academician knows what he is doing. Only colleagues from within the discipline can legitimately question his competence. The ascriptive nature of the academician's posture allows each individual to judge how he should use his time. Consequently, a faculty member can rightfully claim the prerogative of selecting within his area of specialization the content and method for the courses he will teach and the topics he will research.

The independent, holistic, and ascriptive aspects of academic performance influence the academician's sense of institutional propriety and, therefore, the politics of the college in which he works. An examination of these characteristics will constitute the core of this study. The attributes of academic work have been noted by others. J. Victor

Baldridge and his associates see the university as ambiguous in its goals, dominated by its professionalism, and vulnerable to its social environment.[8] From the standpoint of the process of the institution, what Baldridge really says is that a university consists of a collection of individuals who somehow produce a joint product while operating in a highly independent fashion. All activity is organized around the practitioner's academic discipline. Because of the style of academic performance, the academician is inclined to see all collectives as threats to his free pursuit, whether they be the institution within which he himself operates or some other group from the larger society. Thus, the academician has a sense of vulnerability.

Only under extreme provocation will academicians band together to contest the transgressions of outside forces. To do so diverts them from their chosen and independently pursued activities. Even the coming together in a concerted cause for purposes of defending their individual freedom constitutes a threat to their preferred style of performance insofar as it requires them to respond as a group and therefore to accept direction imposed by considerations extraneous to their self-selected areas of teaching and research.

A question that quickly arises is whether a single view of an academician can be applied to those associated with institutions as different as the major graduate schools and the four-year teaching colleges. These structural designators seem to connote different types of academicians. The former will presumably have a preponderance of scholars of some reputation, whereas the latter can be staffed largely by teachers who perform satisfactorily in the classroom but display a low commitment to professional growth within their academic specialties. If a difference exists, it may be in how each responds to the world of ideas. And if there is a similarity, it will be in their sense of creativity. Looking beyond the handful of prestigious graduate schools, it is apparent that academicians at four-year colleges do experience creativity, but that they associate it as much with their teaching as with their publishing. It does not happen every day and in every class, but teaching can provide the intellectual stimulation of creativity that goes beyond the exhilaration of a good exchange with students and the knowledge that teaching has resulted in learning.

The idea that faculty teach only so that students can learn involves the concept of high institutional commitment, with emphasis on service to a clientele, much as in a business endeavor. Creativity, on the other hand, reflects the belief that a product has worth independent of its market value. Faculty at times determine curriculum content totally independent of student wishes. They teach courses with little regard for enrollment, that is, for how well the course "sells," simply because the material being taught is part of a coherent expression of an academic discipline. And they achieve satisfaction from this expression. In such cases, academicians are acting independently of market value. They may be attempting to be creative, or at least to imitate and, therefore, to reminisce about the creativity of those who taught them in graduate school. Even then, there is an association with the creative.

The problem with the teaching variety of creativity is that it is ephemeral. It leaves no monument; it is witnessed only by students, and they may not always appreciate it. In this sense the creative experience is incomplete. The important point, however, is that teaching can constitute an independent and holistic performance characterized by creativity just as scholarship does. Usually it is sanctioned ascriptively by certification in an academic discipline just as much as the authorship that is associated with scholarly writing. From a political standpoint, the teaching academician can be as concerned as the scholar with protecting his ascriptively assigned role as a historian, biologist, or philosopher. He is equally dedicated to preserving within the university the structure and process that support individual expression. To this extent, his political attitudes, as well as the political processes of the institution he inhabits, have much in common with those of the publishing scholar at the prestigious graduate school.

The reward structure of a college also supports the academician's inclination toward creativity. Most academicians see rewards only partially as increased income derived from promotion. Moreover, rank itself gives the academician little sense of authority over others. In this respect it is unlike the higher reaches of a bureaucracy or corporation, where position affords a chief of government or industry direct supervisory responsibilities and the sense of personal power that may go with them. Academia does, however, allow for prerogatives, and within a college these are typically extended in the form of sabbaticals, decreased teaching loads, greater latitude in course selection, and institutional support for an individual's nonteaching activities. In brief, prerogatives are fashioned in ways that allow personal freedom. Pursuit of such freedom suggests that the power of the academician is in personal performance—in individual capacity within his chosen intellectual field.

Even at the four-year teaching colleges rewards are disproportionately associated with a concern for the individual professor's use of time, a commodity that has traditionally been seen as being necessary for intellectual work. When faculty are released from the duties of the classroom, the justification is usually to allow time for scholarship. A few local faculty superstars can be rewarded for teaching performance and even fewer for service to the university, but throughout academia a common theme serves as the foundation for rewards and as the basis for political norms. That theme is some small claim to individual creativity.

But is this description of academia as an independent, holistic, and ascriptive pursuit dedicated to creativity true of the applied disciplines—agriculture, business, and engineering—as well as the arts and sciences? Probably more than some might expect. The work of Everett C. Ladd, Jr., and Seymour Martin Lipset demonstrates that the type of institution with which an academician is affiliated, his academic discipline, and the extent of his personal achievement in research will influence his political views on such matters as faculty unionism and liberal causes.[9] But there are also unifying themes that cut across the lines imposed by institution, discipline, and research. Creativity need not always be considered in esoteric terms. When academicians focus on the implicit aspects of education—doing something that is intellectually satisfying for its own sake—and when they work toward a mental change in themselves as well as in their students, they are headed in the direction of both creativity and the conditions that are likely to generate the attitudes toward a university that will be described in subsequent chapters. In determining the applicability of this explanation of academia and its politics to one academic discipline or another, it is only necessary to decide when the qualities of creativity or the understanding of the implicit meaning of education are sufficiently prevalent among faculty to influence the nature of that particular educational enterprise.

It is in this relationship among creativity, the academician, and the institution by which the academician is employed that we see the meaning of the assertion that the faculty is the university. Without creativity, faculty lose this claim to identity and predominance. An important element of their political strength is thereby sacrificed. Admissions policies have an important part, of course, in shaping the character of any university. In the great leveling of open admissions, the academician can be reduced to little more than his pretensions. But these are important. They often are enough to sustain the academic attitude. However he might be compelled to spend his time, pretensions can assure that the academician will continue to define his role to some extent as a creative one.

Finally, we come to the last of the academician's defenses: Can anything as uncertain as creativity be held accountable under society's ideas of efficiency? Popular support for creativity occurs largely as an article of faith. Whatever the intentions of the practitioner, some ventures will be unproductive. That gamble, in fact, is the excitement (and disillusionment) of creativity. When the academician contends that new ideas can eventually be found in seeming failure, when he argues that close monitoring of his efforts only smothers whatever spark of ingenuity he might otherwise generate, when the weak and sterile academician demands the same collegial treatment as the strong and productive scholar, the administrators of a university can indeed become cynical. They might even accuse the academician of attempting to convert the university into "the faculty's sandbox."

One means of resolving the controversy does exist, but it would be far-reaching: creativity could be franchised and preserved in special sanctuaries at our great research universities. Other strata of higher education would be devoted to teaching and would be managed accordingly. Efficient use of resources would be their badge. But of what use is creativity if it takes place in isolation? Must it reach the public only as a secondhand product dispensed by professional purveyors? The benefits of having creativity in our midst as an element of a community probably outweigh the material savings of conducting it only in special cost-free environments. Even if we attempted to license creativity in this way, it would still occur sub rosa at other places, including the four-year teaching college. But secretive creativity would also be ignored and in part stifled by such a constricted setting. The surrounding community would be the loser.

Perhaps somewhere an institutional arrangement exists which inspires managers to become public advocates of the creativity realized from academic independence. This approach can produce benefits for a university. By appealing to the academician's sense of creativity, the manager would, in fact, be utilizing the academician's own symbols. Ensuing discussion would relate to the meaning of the profession as measured in the exercise of intellect rather than self-interest as measured with material reward. Possibly, it is only in this way that managers can avoid a reconciliation of the two worlds on the basis of the academician's surrendering his own values and begrudgingly accepting in their place the idea of pluralistic competition for re-sources. In our open society such contests have produced little more than a ravenous appetite for consumption. This study is presented in the spirit of explaining the academician's endeavors in a light that might contribute to administrative environments that are conducive to encouraging creativity and scholarship.

2

The Dependent Entrepreneur:
Individual Performance in Academia

Autonomy has long been the concept used to distinguish the relationship of a self-regulated academic department with the larger institution of the university. The individual academician's role has customarily been cloaked in academic freedom. But over the years, the term autonomy has come to be applied to the individual as well—an extension in the academician's view of his rightful independence. Perhaps the most widely accepted definition of academic freedom stipulates that freedom for the professoriate in research is subject to the adequate performance of other duties, and freedom in the classroom is limited by the obligation to exercise care so as not to introduce controversial material unrelated to the area of instruction.[1] The individual autonomy of the professoriate does not include the provisos of this definition. In one extreme formulation that sanctions almost total independence, autonomy has been defined as the antithesis of diversion from or obstruction to an academician's chosen activities.[2] The assertion has been made that the individual must be free from any force that would distort the process of rational discussion. In applying this maxim, only the individual academician can say when he is experiencing such pressure.[3]

One observer noted that some academicians believe the doctrine of academic freedom, as extended into autonomy, confers on them the right to act as if they are self-employed men of property in a laissez-faire system.[4] Clark Kerr has labeled this version of laissez-faire a bizarre result of the German model of a university that revolves around the professor and the classroom and allows faculty the freedom to choose the courses to be taught.[5] Justification for autonomy's central position in higher education rests on the importance of individual freedom to creativity in academic performance. Individual pursuit, so the argument goes, is a necessary source of the critical temper that is vital to the advancement of knowledge. Effectiveness in teaching and scholarship, an academician will maintain, requires that he not be restrained. He must have freedom to develop his talents and capabilities in his own way and at his own pace. He should not be controlled or closely supervised in either his research or his classroom presentations. The underlying assumption is that this freedom results in a diversity that functions to the advantage of students, the university, and higher education. In this image, the university becomes a group of philosophically resourceful professors freed of any constraint (except to please fellow practitioners of their discipline) and told to follow their inquiries wherever these may lead.

The only qualifications to this formulation of the academic career today are that the academician must vigorously engage in intellectual activity of his choosing and share the university's instructional burden by accepting an equitable proportion of students. In some cases he must also teach certain established material. Academicians contend, however, that even these limitations can be legitimately imposed only at the level of the discipline-oriented department. Beyond the department, corporate responsibility becomes a hazy concept in the mind of the classic academician.

To the extent that this hypothetical autonomy appropriately applies to an academic career, it probably relates to only one specific pursuit—the creation and teaching of philosophical truths. Yet, the concept has been adapted to all teaching of all types of courses. Jacques Barzun, who used the term "individualization of faculty," pointed out that the occurrence of autonomy dates from the post World War II era of intensive academic specialization.[6] The academician's autonomy, however, has a much longer tradition in Western practice. Essentially, it is individualism of an old and extreme form, being composed for a person who wishes to devote his life to the cultivation of his own reason.[7] In this sense, René Descartes may be viewed as the first modern academician, not from the standpoint of teaching but of style—the manner in which he approached his work. Six principles characterize the Cartesian approach:

1. Intellectual activity should be pursued individually and independently.

> ...truths [Descartes said]...are much more likely to be found by one man than by a whole people.[8]

2. There can be no limit on inquiry.

I resolved to go slowly and...to seek the true method of arriving at knowledge of everything my mind was capable of grasping.[9]

3. Rational consideration is universal.

But what satisfied me the most about this method was that, through it, I was assured of using my reason in everything.[10]

4. The scholar should have objectivity—a certain detachment from the situation to which he is applying his reason.

I did nothing but wander here and there in the world, trying to be spectator rather than actor in all the comedies which were being played there....[R]eflecting particularly in each matter on what might render it doubtful and give occasion for error, I rooted out from my mind, during this time, all errors that had introduced themselves into it hitherto.[11]

5. Personal calculations of a scholar must always be made to amplify the time allowed for scholarship.

Moreover, I did not wish to begin to reject completely any of the opinions which might have slipped earlier into my mind without having been introduced by reason, until I had first given myself enough time to make a plan of the work I was undertaking.[12]

6. A secure and stable environment is essential to the cultivation of reason.

It is exactly eight years since this wish [to be worthy of his learned reputation] made me decide to leave all those places where I had acquaintances, and to withdraw here to a country where the long duration of the war has established such discipline that the armies maintained there [*sic*] seem to serve only to ensure that the fruits of peace are enjoyed with the maximum of security; and where, in the midst of a great crowd of busy people, more concerned with their own business than curious about that of others, without lacking any conveniences offered by the most populous cities, I have been able to live as solitary and withdrawn as I would in the most remote of deserts.[13]

In this formulation implied by Descartes more than three centuries ago, we find the essence of the academician's autonomy. Descartes's method will be used in this study as the normative foundation of academic attitudes—the test for academic genuineness. The characterization of the academician as a contemporary Cartesian is not meant to apply, however, to more than the method our first academician gave us. Other aspects of his thinking may not be appropriate for the philosophical bent of any particular academician.

Manipulating Independence

In considering academic problems in Chapter 1, performance was seen to be independent, ascriptive, and holistic. The academician does not work in the same differentiated and therefore interdependent way as someone in industry or a bureaucracy. But he is subjected to institutional discipline of a sort. Rather than being differentiated, academic activity is segmented. A limited body of material is considered by a single professor performing a discrete function of instruction or research. Another academician may devote time to related material, but he will do so in an entirely independent fashion. Segmented performance allows the practitioner to avoid many of the constraints normally associated with the operations of an organization because one individual's daily routine is not bound to that of others. Once a course is assigned, the academician need be concerned with colleagues only to the extent that class schedules must be coordinated. In teaching and research, he may digress for a day, a week, or even a month without colleagues and administrators knowing or usually caring. Even the exact content of the course is left to the instructor. In considering the academician in this chapter, we will see that not just the style of performance, but also perceptions of the college and how it functions are shaped to place professors beyond the constraints that are normally imposed on those who work in a joint enterprise. The defense of independence—the self-selection of professional activities—is the primary political purpose of the academician.

Higher education as a product in our society has a comprehensive quality insofar as the sum of the courses of which a college degree is comprised relates to some objective of the degree's recipient. When assembled and labeled as a Bachelor of Arts or Science degree, a group of courses is accepted as something rational. But this unity is not supplied by the academician. It must be provided by the student himself. The professoriate merely imparts the pieces of the product. The consumer, so to speak, achieves the synthesis which a degree in business, primary education, engineering, or sociology represents. The academician resists this task because it suggests that considerations external, and perhaps even contradictory, to his chosen mission may define his purpose and determine how he will use his time. As a synthesizer, he would be required to assume a closer relationship with students. Interdependence would creep into the academic pursuit. Its purpose would shift from faculty creativity to student learning, the focus much of the public mistakenly believes is at the bottom of all activity of faculty in a university or college. Thus, we have our first glimpse of the basic tension that exists between academia and the society from which it emanates.

Because of the low interdependence among faculty, the academician's attachment to his research or his students can become paramount. But freedom is the foundation of all relationships. As a teacher, the academician regulates his relations with students. Segmented performance and the refusal to be drawn into the task of providing an overarching synthesis for a student's degree clearly give the sense of working alone that is found in Descartes's first principle.

The additional factor of voluntarism may be as important as working individually and independently. In an academician's association with students, each must be free to reject the other. In a somewhat idealized version of higher education, Robert Wolff sees academia as a place where an aspiring student practices an enterprise under the guidance of a scholar. Any submission to authority is free, voluntary, and revokable.[14] The academician's autonomy is protected by allowing the student the option of withdrawing from the relationship. Without this opportunity for egress, students might remain to press unusual demands upon the professor.

The noteworthy aspect of the academician's autonomy is that it provides a basis for his activities devoid of the constraints of social structure. Society virtually drops from the picture, and we are left with a world of symbols. Daniel Bell has said that a university is a place where people feel an attachment to something beyond themselves—scholarship, learning, books, ideas, the past.[15] Perhaps inadvertently, Bell captured the essence of academic autonomy in this statement. It is not human association alone which is an academician's concern, but human association in abstract values. Social structure becomes secondary just as it did for Descartes when he behaved as a spectator rather than an actor. Only by ignoring society and its vicissitudes can an academician capture the objectivity (the detachment) of the fourth Cartesian principle—the need to enhance reason. It is widely recognized that universities have tended to be insulated from the direct influence of many social demands. Thus the characterization of academia as an ivory tower. In this regard, a basis for acknowledging differences between academia and our pluralistic society is well established.

The outside observer who is attempting to grasp the meaning of academic behavior experiences a dilemma that can be explained by Herbert Simon's inner and outer environment.[16] In total innocence, the outsider may examine the functions of a university in an effort to understand the academic profession. But functions reveal only how the university relates to (and serves) society—its outer environment. They tell us very little about the internal environment of the institution, that is, the inner workings of the academic community which the functions sustain.

It is indeed difficult to imagine an institution without some structure. In academia this structure is present in the discipline of the practitioner, the convention of face-to-face contact with a certain number of students, and an understanding that a teacher will instruct in predetermined areas thereby giving some semblance of logic to the university's course offerings. In the normal sense, however, there need not be a compelling logic in the institutional relationships of faculty members. To the extent that interdependence exists in a university, it is affective—a sense of being together in a shared culture. No clear image of the institution's structure emerges from this characterization. The importance the academician places on autonomy suggests that from his standpoint, the less structure the better.

The academician, in effect, hopes to conduct his affairs in an institution that does not really have the attributes of an institution. The university carries the ideal of low power orientation, if not the obliteration of power altogether. Each scholar, following his individual pursuits, has little use for jurisdiction over others. His rewards do not come from institutional authority but from work in his discipline. Colleagues who seek power—except in the most benign manner and then only to broaden options for the department or occasionally for the faculty as a whole—are deprecated as local politicians. Administrators who overtly exercise power are viewed with suspicion, and their efforts at rationalizing institutional relationships are opposed. In such a role, administrators are, after all, attempting to place constraints upon the individual that limit his freedom. In taking this step they behave contrary to an important feature of the academic culture.

Robert Wolff concluded that because of the nature of the educational function, academia cannot be governed.[17] It is probably not possible to come any closer to a determinant in academic politics than through the view of authority which this assertion implies. This view marks the essential difference between pluralistic and academic politics.

The Burden of Comparison

These perceptions produce an unusual condition for academia—competition becomes muted. The norms of academic behavior, it seems, preclude professional rivalry from being treated in a good-natured fashion. The position is commonly taken that teaching and personally directed intellectual activity in search of enlightenment validate comparison only against an individual's own previous best efforts. At Harvard such a situation occurred in 1977 when students suggested that the college give an award for outstanding teaching to one professor each year. The faculty council rejected the proposal.[18] Even such limited competition as singling out one person from among the entire faculty could not be tolerated. Whereas competitiveness can be a potent incentive when mutually desired rewards are allocated on the basis of efficiency, it cannot become an acknowledged factor in group relationships if personal comparisons are discouraged. Academic life, therefore, is characterized by the lack of any direct measure of relative worth. When comparison does take place, it is seen by the individual who is being compared as proceeding in an atmosphere meant to culminate in either total acceptance or total rejection.

In an institutional sense, comparison means evaluation, and in academia this does not come easy. Particularly in the evaluation of teaching is there an air of decorum and propriety. Outsiders—the uninitiated—must respect the individual scholar's claim to special competence in his sphere of activity, and this prescription extends to colleagues engaged in other disciplines. General classroom competence is assessed only through the campus grapevine, an occasional stab at student evaluation of teaching, or the impressions of peers. The reputation among colleagues for being a good teacher rests principally on the attitude of an academician toward his classes and his material. It derives from self-reporting. If a teacher returns from a class to express enthusiasm to an office mate over how well things went that day, and occasionally when he seems truly concerned because he senses that he has failed to reach the students in a particular session, the conclusion of peers is that "old Shivley is a good teacher," Over the years, as the various sources of information tend to corroborate one another, a reputation is established. Esteem is often built upon the most meager of direct evidence, and the entire issue of how good a particular member of the faculty is as a teacher can remain shrouded in mystery. Seldom does evidence exist with regard to a professor's teaching that can be used by a college to demonstrate that a particular academician is a poor teacher. In the meantime, presumptions favor the individual practitioner of the art. He is assumed to be satisfactory in the classroom.

Formal evaluation is generally conducted with a questionnaire that is distributed to students toward the end of a course. Classroom visitation by peers may also be used. Then there is evaluation by chairmen and administrators. But college teachers prefer to avoid the matter altogether. Outside evaluation is the beginning of external controls, which in the minds of most academicians are contrary to the Cartesian principles and the independence these allow. Surveys on higher education that have touched on this matter find that student evaluations are challenged by most faculty as being ineffective because they cannot possibly assess the purpose of the classroom, which is expressing creativity. Academicians will maintain that only peers within their discipline can legitimately evaluate their performance.[19] Yet, classroom observation by peers will be resisted. The argument can be made that the evaluator may not favor the pedagogical style of the evaluated, and who is to say which style is more effective? Whatever the experts on teaching might say, most academicians maintain that quality in classroom performance is very subjective, a question of preference. One style is not necessarily superior to another.

Beyond this point, various means of evaluation that might be used have few faculty advocates. Highly structured systems consisting of questionnaires are seen as being overly mechanical, impersonal, and without merit. When faculty do devise a form to be used by students or for purposes of assessment by a chairman, a dean, or a department evaluation committee, they often shape it to conceal rather than reveal information about what takes place in the classroom. Many faculty opt, for example, for fewer rather than for more gradations of peformance. A three-level scale of "outstanding," "commendable," and "marginal" is preferred to a five- or seven-level scale that conveys more information.

The purpose of academicians, of course, is to make it more difficult for evaluators to draw distinctions among them. In extreme cases, departments have proposed that student evaluations of teaching not use scales at all. Rather, each student should be allowed to write a paragraph on the instructor's performance. Tabulation and comparison of faculty then become virtually impossible. Not just the weaker members of a department take this approach. The concealing of weakness in performance is not always the point. Those having an affinity for the academic culture generally question the legitimacy of comparisons among individuals. The Cartesian's first principle is that his work has nothing to do with others, that "truths...are much more likely to be found by one man than by a whole people." An individual can be evaluated only on his own merits, the academician contends. A scholar's worth is absolute and intrinsic; it cannot be assessed against the relative performance of other faculty members, particularly if they are concerned with dissimilar disciplinary pursuits.

Comparison with others is not acceptable because it is a means of arriving at an institutional judgment. As such, it can be used to control, perhaps even to modify, an individual's performance by holding up the techniques and practices of faculty who have higher evaluation ratings as a model for those colleagues who have been adjudged as less capable. Comparative evaluation, therefore, becomes the antithesis of academic autonomy. If student evaluation is to be used at all, many contend, it should be seen only by the evaluated to use as "feedback"— a device for self-improvement. Evaluation in this view can have no institutional purpose.

As an evaluator of peers, the academician exhibits the same perception as when he himself is the subject of evaluation. But comparisons of one colleague with another cannot always be avoided. Several peers may be eligible for promotion, for example, while budgetary constraints limit recognition to a few. In such cases, elaborate schemes are devised to conceal as much of the judgment as possible. As department committees are called upon to assess peers for promotion, they sometimes recommend all who apply or are nominated. They distinguish among candidates only to the extent of indicating a preference by listing them in order of priority, and then with the pious hope that all will be promoted. The language used to make distinctions among the recommendations can become so convoluted that it is difficult for readers to determine who is really being recommended. Somehow this approach seems to absolve the evaluators of any responsibility when a colleague is not promoted. In effect, an administrator, perhaps with the advice of an extradepartmental committee of faculty, must make the actual choice. The final decision may amount to little more than a confirmation of a department committee's actual preference. Nevertheless, when the judgment is reached, peers from within the department can contend that they did not compare colleagues. Even then, there is a certain uneasiness among evaluators over the possibility of a peer discovering how he was ranked.

When serving on evaluation committees outside their departments, academicians may not be so sensitive about making comparisons, but even at this level, curious things happen. When a candidate's name is presented for consideration, evaluators will defer to anyone among their number who is from the candidate's discipline. Only he possesses the ascriptive truth of the same terminal degree that may even remotely allow for evaluation. Committee members will also insist that all material that reflects relative ratings assigned to candidates be destroyed after decisions are made. Only a final recommendation for or against the promotion to be made by a dean, vice-president, or president remains, and a purposeful air of uncertainty is sometimes created over whether the administrator has followed the advice of the faculty committee. In this way, the academician is relieved of the anguish of having compared one colleague with another.

Formal evaluation within an institutional context is clearly a concept alien to the academic culture. Its application to university relationships in recent years is a measure of the success of pluralistic society in imposing its standards on the academy. Many academicians would somehow prefer that a few distinguished and beloved (that is, nonthreatening) senior colleagues gather and decide that it is time for Jones to be promoted but Borkowski can wait until next year. Signals are meant to be subtle in such determinations, and agreements are often reached without anything specific having been said about either one candidate or another, or about the necessity to preserve a balance in distributing rewards among departments. The entire process would take place without yearly ratings, student evaluations, or other paraphernalia that allow for comparisons. The extent to which a faculty holds this preference for apportioning rewards tells us something about the academician's view of community.

Curiously, the stigma of comparing colleagues is not attached to voting for peers who are nominated for college or even for department committee assignments. The distinction may be that such matters pertain to college governance and are not a direct measure of professionalism implicit in assessing a colleague's practice of his discipline.

Somewhere between the two perceptions is the election of department chairmen. At times, divisiveness over which candidate is worthy is sharp and direct. In other cases, intricate systems are devised that include voting for more than one candidate and using complex point systems. Ultimately, someone gets the most points and is elected chairman, but the score sheets from which the outcome is determined may give few clues as to where the consensus really lay, or if one existed at all. The participants in such a scheme may know exactly whom they want to occupy the chair. But in arriving at the desired result, each must do what he can to avoid the impression of having actually made comparisons and taken part in the implied rejection of those colleagues who were unsuccessful candidates for the post.

Precisely because so few distinctions are made in the judgment of teaching, competition among academicians often centers on other areas. Many faculty are seized with the importance of scholarly recognition as the means by which they are afforded approbation within their discipline. Consequently, contests over rewards sometimes center on published research—one of the few aspects in an academic career that is tangible enough to be evaluated. In this case also, the academician evaluating his peers avoids direct comparisons and personal judgments. Assessments of publications are based upon such external or secondary criteria as reviews of a candidate's books, his success in publishing articles in highly respected journals, and his election to honorific societies. Comparisons are avoided to the extent that the judgments of third parties are accepted. The assumption is made that if the editor of a fairly good journal decides to publish an article, it must be good. Seldom do those who rely on such a means of evaluation read the article. At times, a judgment between two candidates for promotion comes down to a comparison of the quality of the journals in which they publish.

All the time these activities are taking place, the academician is left to his individual and holistic pursuits and to the fear that the contest may be unjustly decided against him. If he complains at all, it will not be that he has not been rewarded, but that someone else has. In so doing, he does not appear to be expressing resentment over failure to be recognized. His chagrin is that of having been rejected on the basis of comparison with others. In fact, he is expressing resentment over institutional judgments.

Sometimes when outsiders listen to academicians' complaints they may conclude that college teachers are a naturally mean lot. This is not the case. The trouble is that the independent nature of academic activity leaves the academician with few means of explaining failure. At such times, he is left to his own devices. In order to follow the third Cartesian principle—using his reason in everything—he has chosen to stand apart insofar as reason is the implement of the individual working alone. For someone so dedicated, any hint of rejection touches the very sense of being.

This description of the academic perception shows that there are risks for the individual who chooses to avoid the constraints of an institution—to work in an independent and holistic fashion under an ascriptively ordained position. To the extent that an academician achieves success through public recognition, his glories are his own. He need not share them with others. But in the absence of the acclaim that often passes for success among those engaged in a creative endeavor, there is indeed a sense of loneliness. Perhaps James T. Farrell best captured the essence of the problem in commenting on the experience of a young writer:

> There are moments when he feels himself set against the opposition of the entire world. There are occasions when he turns a caustic wit, a brutal sarcasm, and a savage arrogance on others only because he is defending himself from himself. Suddenly, he will be devastated by an image of himself in which he sees a nobody who has had the temerity and egotism to call himself a writer; i.e., creative. He measures himself, with his few unpublished manuscripts, against the accomplishments of great writers, and his ambition suddenly seems like insanity....A sense of failure dogs his steps.[20]

The academician's quest for personal autonomy not only influences how he sees himself in an institutional setting. It also has a bearing on his attitude toward the university—how it allocates financial resources and how it treats the development of new programs and the formulation of policy. Again, perceptions on these matters rest on the assumption that allowing free inquiry is in the interest of students, the university, and higher education.

Growth and its concomitant, strength, are not associated in the academician's mind with any increase in a college's size as measured in numbers of students. Nor is institutional capability viewed from the standpoint of quantifiable features of a university's output. Rather, growth is seen as enrichment—an extension in institutional potential for satisfying an ever-widening range of intellectual interests. It is an environment that can sustain the application of Descartes's second principle, "arriving at knowledge of everything my mind was capable of grasping." As the academician's mind masters one topic or area of intellectual interest and moves on to another, the university must provide the opportunities that are necessary for exploring the new interests. Otherwise, dissatisfaction will set in, and there is plenty of it at most colleges and universities.

Growth within the academic perception is to be found in more library books, improved professional travel opportunities, new teaching options, and technologically more advanced laboratory equipment. There must be constant growth in the college's capability for extending the intellectual horizons of the individual faculty member. Growth for the sake of growth is a popular goal in pluralistic twentieth-century society. It conveys strength, well-being, and prestige for those who are associated with a prospering institution. This approach has little credence among faculty, however, unless it also accommodates some of their individual concerns. Many academicians simply lack an institutional perspective. They often are highly critical of expenditures for sports and student activities (which do not expand faculty intellectual opportunities) even when these seem to other constituencies of the college to fit harmoniously into institutional growth.

The Politics of Balance

Even though the academician sees growth principally in the ability to sustain intellectual inquiry, the allocation of growth is important to him. This problem receives no more than routine attention in studies of the academic attitude. But when we examine it carefully, we discover that there is a proclivity for balance in all things that impinge upon the academic profession. Most of those who engage in social science research are trained, of course, to make distinctions. They hinge their interpretations on clear preferences that give unusual weight to one factor or another. When they encounter a balance among preferences, those who interpret survey data generally proceed on to some phenomenon that is more dynamic. After all, what can be said about a balanced view in a profession that cherishes harmony and stability? But in the academician's balance of preferences, we encounter something that provides yet additional insight into the politics of this unusual profession.

A survey conducted by Talcott Parsons and Gerald M. Platt among 419 academicians at eight institutions showed faculty to be almost unanimous in asserting that all options that allow for a wider scope of academic inquiry should be available. Few preferences were noted. One of the academician's guiding principles is apparently balance in all things. When queried on an ideal division of time, for example, between teaching and research, respondents in the Parsons and Platt survey overwhelmingly preferred an even allocation between the two pursuits. The same approach characterized their preference for graduate and undergraduate teaching.[21]

A survey by Baldridge and his colleagues yielded this same dedication to balance. This study measured how 9,237 faculty at 249 institutions preferred criteria for promotion and tenure to be weighed. In response to a query regarding how things should be, faculty choice at the public and private multiversities included within the survey was for undergraduate teaching and research to be given roughly the same weight and graduate teaching slightly less. The concept of balance was left generally intact.

In a refinement of his findings, Baldridge reported that only at multiversities, where research was given unusual stress in the apportioning of rewards, did participants in the survey want less emphasis on it. At elite colleges, public comprehensive universities, and public colleges, where research was given consideration along with various types of teaching, faculty were relatively content with the attention afforded it. At private liberal arts colleges, community colleges, and private junior colleges, where virtually no weight is given to research, faculty would have liked it to receive greater consideration.[22] Baldridge's survey pointed, therefore, in the direction of the same unqualified confirmation of the academician's view of balance as Parsons and Platt's. Whatever their condition, academicians apparently hope to move away from extremes and toward an equilibrium among the forces that influence their well-being.

And what are we to make of these data? The balanced response does not necessarily indicate the individual academician's preference. But it does protect his political position. Decisions on changes in an academic program are often taken at the institutional level based on the combination and weights that provide the greatest advantage to the university as a whole. Necessarily, such decisions take preferences into account and measure one activity against another. They thus have the potential for limiting the choice of the individual academician. An important aspect of choice is the necessity to reserve it. Protection of the academician's independence often requires, therefore, that he give a "nonanswer" to such questions as those asked by Parsons and Platt or by Baldridge.

In one category, however, a clear preference was expressed in the Baldridge survey. At colleges and public comprehensive universities, undergraduate teaching was seen as being more important in assessing performance than either research or graduate teaching. But Baldridge conceded that the same academicians who opt for emphasis on teaching in promotion and tenure opposed student evaluations and challenged their validity when the results are used to deny recognition and reward!

And how is this response to be interpreted? One possibility is that at the colleges and universities of these respondents insufficient acclaimed research and graduate instruction (essentially supervision of Ph.D. dissertations) was being performed to allow all faculty to be assessed similarly when it came to promotions. If evaluators were permitted to use research and graduate instruction in assessments of faculty, they could make distinctions. The respondents' answers protected everyone and thereby actually showed a proclivity for balance. Research and graduate education are sufficiently common to constitute norms (and provide balance) only at the multiversity. In effect, the faculty at colleges and regular universities were also providing "nonanswers" in favoring a heavier weight for teaching. Then, too, as long as student evaluation of teaching can be avoided, why not use teaching as the criterion for reward?

Moving on from preferences in the use of their time to the means employed to allocate resources, we find academicians acknowledging that in some disciplines they require more resources than in others to accomplish their objectives. The natural sciences, technical areas, and the arts—the "hands-on" programs—need more equipment and supplies than the humanities and most social sciences. This consideration is factored into the academician's concept of balance. The question is not one of all disciplines having the same, but is a matter of each academician having enough to pursue whatever his mind is capable of grasping. Academicians carry this ethos even further. If resources are limited, each should still receive an allocation that reflects some measure of need even though under extreme conditions this approach could mean that satisfactory work could not be conducted in any single discipline. The hard choice by which one program is eliminated to protect the integrity of others is seldom made. Thus, we see the meaning of harmony in serving as the community dynamic within the academic culture.

Scarcity—Resources and Time

In a survey of more than 1,200 individuals at fifteen universities, Paul Dressel and his associates developed data on how academicians respond to the relationship among disciplines. When confronted with the question of whether departmental autonomy leads to the type of resource commitment which precludes rational planning in allocating for the university as a whole, 27 percent of the subjects gave no response, 7 percent claimed not to understand the question or believed themselves unqualified to answer it, and 6 percent said they were uncertain. The issue was evaded, therefore, by 40 percent of respondents. An additional 30 percent answered in the negative.[23] These two categories represented an amazing 70 percent of the participants in the survey who could not relate to the financial corporative judgment that is the key to resource allocation and power relationships in so much of the private and public life of our society.

In effect, academia has only a poorly developed concept of scarcity. To acknowledge scarcity is to concede that choices can be made and that limitations can be placed on the pursuit of knowledge. Faculty must resist the assumptions of this possibility. A comparative judgment is seldom made, therefore, between the relative advantages of two programs that may be competing for funds. The inclination is to consider programs in the same way that colleagues are assessed—"on their merits." Good ideas abound, and each incorporates some benefit. The academic program-building process tends, therefore, to pyramid one activity atop another, always in the name of enrichment. A program's rationale is easily lost, and for the efficiency-minded manager, the result is unnecessary proliferation.

Academicians, including deans and vice-presidents whose earlier experience was in the classroom, often express an inclination for what an outsider can only consider as the mindless addition of new degree opportunities. More often than not, growth within the university is measured solely in number of new programs. At first, this approach seems quantitative insofar as new programs will supposedly attract additional students. But this conclusion is open to question. Additional programs simply allow new options for students who would attend the university anyway. They also serve the academician's desire for an ever-expanding intellectual universe. Proliferation is abetted by the academic sense that for all intellectual activity, legitimacy derives simply from the fact that a program exists. It is not tied in any way to the immediate benefit that the university or society actually receives from it. If the question of program legitimacy is even raised in university circles, it is invariably dismissed with the assertion that the institution can only benefit from offering students more options. A problem develops only when scarcity occurs—when new options must be pursued without additions to university income. At this point, all programs suffer privation under the academician's system.

Yet another Cartesian principle is concealed in the academician's concept of balance—the veneration of time. Even Descartes's phrasing of the fifth principle suggests the independence of the scholar in the use of his time—"Moreover, I did not wish to begin...until I had first given myself enough time to make a plan of the work I was undertaking."[24] No outside agent intercedes in this concept of the relationship between the academician and his time. Time, in fact, is the currency of the academician. If an economics for academia based on calculations of time does not exist, one could surely be invented because it exists in the mind of every academician.

Someone who sees intellectual activity as an individual endeavor, who resists any limitation on inquiry, and whose profession rests upon the pursuit of whatever knowledge his mind is capable of grasping will naturally insist upon controlling the use of his own time. Preventing increases in the teaching load is central to all considerations, whether the new demands concern class size, contact hours, or course offerings. Not being a member of a truly hierarchical structure, the academician has no way of delegating newly assigned tasks. Being unable to pass them on, he must attempt to avoid them altogether insofar as they can place a claim on his time.

The problem is not simply the amount of time demanded from faculty. Any rigid plan for scheduling time also limits a faculty member's preferences and is considered undesirable. This issue can arise, for example, when universities attempt to program resources more tightly and strive for more efficient use of space by insisting that classes be scheduled from 8:00 A.M. to 10:00 P.M. rather than some time between 10:00 A.M. and 2:00 P.M. when the faculty would rather teach. The academician also sees any request to teach outside his discipline as an unnatural demand on him insofar as time is being taken from his preferred activities. In this regard, specified general education courses that are somewhat removed from the discipline can become a source of discontent for faculty.

This reverence for time can be a fiction. Some academicians are involved in "schoolteaching." Selling real estate, playing the stock market (for the more affluent), moonlighting at a nearby community college, or simply a life of leisure will have precedence over the lonely pursuit of knowledge. Others will claim, and no doubt with a great deal of justification, that they are not interested in the scholarly attainment found in publication or in professional activity as consultants, speakers, and the like. Theirs is the world of books—intellectual development in the broad but personal experience of literature, biography, or philosophical issues. Their time is used accordingly. An administrator is thereupon left with the dilemma of assessing the worth of each professor's activity. And seldom can the product be measured. Are courses really better because of this freedom? The academician has preserved a relationship with society that may find its roots in the medieval church—he is supported in exchange for ministering to the intellect (rather than to the spirit). No further precision or definition is possible. An important part of the bargain involves the unfettered use of time.

Curiosities of Academic Policy

Robert Wolff's observation that an educational establishment cannot be governed has already been noted. To the extent that faculty rule out interdisciplinary comparisons and operate with the perception of balance in apportioning time and resources, the observation becomes apparent. This attitude has profound implications for educational policy. Policy, of course, implies some overarching theme or sense of direction governing group activities. Responsibility for such guidance rightfully belongs to the faculty, it can be argued, because education is essentially a relationship between faculty and students. It is the relationship of the professional looking after the uninitiated or perhaps a novice. The instructor assumes responsibility for policy because he is the guardian of competence and integrity in professional standards as they apply to his discipline. No administrator can serve this purpose.

Within academia, standards are grounded in the meaning of a resource's use rather than in the efficiency of its use. The academic purpose is to make each act a policy unto itself. But as unusual as this idea might seem, is it really surprising for a profession that insists upon intellectual activity being pursued individually and independently? The third Cartesian principle—to apply reason to everything—is really an individual's statement. Policy is an institutional perception that ultimately might contradict the individual's use of reason. Thus policy is often ignored by the academician.

The implication of the academic perception is that there can be no policy. In this regard, Clark Kerr has interpreted the elective system, which allows students to select their courses, as a means of lifting from faculty the burden of policy, that is, determining what an education should include.[25] Distribution requirements in a program of study have much the same effect. In the name of educational breadth there is balance; students are exposed equally to each area into which knowledge has been compartmentalized. In a general education or core program, embellishments are sometimes added in order to liken the results to a microcosm of a cultured person's experience in the universe. In any case, balance is assured. In discussing the matter, Martin Trow observed approvingly that whatever its failures, this approach to general education reduces the amount of academic decision making—almost as if avoiding a decision (and policy) is virtuous.[26] Policy, therefore, follows institutional structure into the realm of the unimportant. The purposes of academic autonomy are served.

On occasion the academician finds that he has gone too far in neglecting policy and in permitting the obliteration of academic structure. This phenomenon was seen in the onslaught against course requirements during the late 1960s as colleges opted for the innovation of a student-oriented and "relevant" curriculum. In furthering student choice, a number of curriculum desiderata were set aside—foreign language, history, distribution requirements, sometimes a specified general education program, and even structure in major areas of study.

With the end of requirements, many academicians found that the liberated student was no longer being channeled automatically into their courses in a balanced fashion. Small enrollments were seen as the stigma of not being sought after by students for whatever reason. Often without recognizing the source of the problem, academicians began to compete with one another for students, even while they continued to castigate the evils of requirements and to praise the individualized programs students were permitted to devise for themselves. The most obvious sign of this development was the appearance of flashy course titles such as "Big Brother: 1974 + 10 = ?" rather than "Totalitarianism," which is standard sociological fare. The titles were meant to attract students, but they also debased the profession and appeared ludicrous on a transcript. And what was the source of all this nonsense? The academician failed to recognize the purpose of policy or its relationship to an organization's operations. Free-floating individuals did not make a university after all.

By the late 1970s, with the heyday of sensational experientialism behind them, faculty again came to recognize that program requirements for students did not limit the academician's independence. Rather, it spared him the instability which Descartes saw as being antithetical to the cultivation of reason. It lessened the paronoia of open competition and invidious comparison that is contrary to the norms of the academician's culture. In retrospect, the trend away from structure could be seen as an outside force that compelled the academician to modify his behavior in order to accommodate a passing perception of our open society. In the final analysis, program structure proved to be more than a means of providing a student with breadth and depth in education. It preserved the academician's balanced approach and constituted a device that he could not easily surrender. Only with a well-defined policy meant to be observed by all could the academician's purposes be met. But here we see another academic practice. Policy is phrased as a norm, a passive device of social control. A norm is meant to be observed, not enforced. Thus, the academician is left free from the constraint of the institution which policy implies.

Even with the passing of the campus hysteria of the 1960s, the tension between the society and the academy over institutional policy was not ended. As student demands for relevancy faded, colleges were seized by an atmosphere of careerism, a reflection of society's new mood. With it came the professional accrediting agencies, which attempted to dictate curriculum content in such areas as social work, business, technology, and nursing. Before a program would be sanctified, certain requirements had to be met. Generally, these were so numerous, but yet so narrow, that they contradicted the idea of providing all students with the breadth of knowledge found in the humanities, arts, and social sciences of general education.

At first, the source of the onslaught was not properly identified. The accrediting agencies were in the hands of educators who were ascriptively ordained by advanced degrees. They appeared to be academicians themselves. The rise of the accreditors was seen as an effort of disciplines to police themselves. Faculties of the applied disciplines that were moving in this direction became staunch supporters of the accrediting agencies' demands and maintained that the general education portions of the curriculum must be reduced or modified to accommodate them. But ultimately it could be seen that the new development was another encroachment by society upon the academy. Students and their parents developed a preoccupation with assuring that their school or program was properly accredited. This mood reflected the perception of a bureaucratized society seeking individual certification for future employment rather than education for all of life's pursuits. Many college officials moved willingly with the current, giving little thought to its meaning or origin. An outside force was attempting to determine policy within the university. The academician again came within a hair's breadth of losing control of his university. And all because he failed to understand the implications of policy.

Academia's Paradox

The concepts that have been explored in this chapter—avoiding evaluation and comparisons, working for balance in all things, preserving independence in the use of time, and negating policy and even authority in the univeristy—all contribute to the stable environment which the academician seeks under the sixth Cartesian principle. It is the same stability that Descartes sought when he withdrew to Holland, where armies had imposed a discipline on the population which ensured the fruits of peace with a maximum of security. The paradox, of course, is that the academician hopes to see conditions imposed on others that will permit him to escape constraints himself. But without social interaction (a force that in most cases is contrary to stability), how can the academician be a part of the society he serves?

The mystery of academia, in fact, is how it manages to flourish in a social setting that would seemingly be hostile to its assumptions. After all, if academicians are not interdependent, neither are they independent. They must have support to pursue their inquiries. Robert Nisbet sees the genius of academia in its management of this dependent state in a manner that allows it near independence in its activities. The academician achieves this feat, Nisbet believes, by intermingling the intellectual aspects of his work with moral and social features to which the larger community can relate.[27] Recent surveys show that in spite of their efforts to place the operation of colleges and universities under greater control, legislators, trustees, and administrators agree (apparently hypothetically) with the assertion that autonomy is essential to intellectual creativity.[28] The academician's value-oriented appeals are partially credible, and if a sufficient number of incantations can be included in academia's conjuring, support will be forthcoming for one reason, if not for another. Furthermore, by resisting organizational structure, the academician can insist that his condition is an individual dependence on his own academic community, and he never asks how or where that community obtains resources to support him.

In this set of relationships, unusual things happen to responsibility. By avoiding power, the academician avoids responsibility. His obligation is to intellectuality—to the dissemination of culture and knowledge. The "academic community," through administrators who work the channels of communications between society and the professoriate, shoulders the responsibility for obtaining from society the resources that will permit academicians to carry on their mission. The academician himself solicits funds directly from the government or foundations, but usually only for his personal research activities. In either case, the recipient enjoys rights without responsibility. He need justify his activities only by his dedication to the advancement of his discipline. Responsibility, after all, incorporates restraint.

A mundane example will demonstrate this point. In both business and government, regular attendance on the job is a basic requirement for continued employment. Attendance is tied directly to remuneration. As surprising as it may seem to outsiders, this link is not always well established in academia. In most colleges, institutional practice allows faculty to be absent from class to attend professional meetings. But faculty sometimes cancel classes on their own initiative for personal reasons as well. Such action is an unstated prerogative derived from the academician's autonomy. The test of the faculty perception on this matter is the response if an administrator questions the action and points to the implied contract into which a college enters when it accepts an enrollment from a student. The meaning of this contract is that some form of instruction, which at least remotely resembles the description of the course printed in the college catalog, will be offered at a specified time and place.

But this is an institutional perception, and many faculty have only a hazy understanding of the suggestion that they are not free to vary the time and place of a class, to talk about whatever they wish, or even to cancel a class when some professional or even personal activity arises which they believe requires their presence elsewhere. Faculty see their position as being protected by a terminal degree and eventually tenure. Nothing else is important. Thereupon, they, and they alone, determine what will take place in the classroom, or, in some cases, if anything will take place. At times, when discussing a particular absence, they will even argue that a student was better off with an individual "library assignment" than with instruction! They can indeed behave as self-employed men of property in a laissez-faire system.

Any academician who takes the time to think about his world will usually uncover many of the themes presented in this chapter. One lucid statement was prepared by F. M. Cornford, the first Laurence Professor of Ancient Philosophy at Cambridge. In a somewhat whimsical piece published in 1908, Cornford saw rapid change as the greatest peril to the things academicians value. For the most part, this change is not caused by academicians themselves but tends to originate outside the college. Cornford tied principle and value to the necessity for stability. "A principle," he said, "is a rule of inaction, which states a valid general reason for not doing in any particular case what, to unprincipled instinct, would appear to be right." Cornford continued, "These principles are all deducible from the fundamental maxim that the first necessity for a body of men engaged in the pursuits of learning is freedom from the burden of political cares. It is impossible to enjoy the contemplation of truth if one is vexed and distracted by the sense of responsibility. Hence the wisdom of our ancestors devised a form of academic polity in which this sense is, so far as human imperfection will allow, reduced to the lowest degree."[29]

Thus we experience the dependent entrepreneur whose watchword is autonomy. He abhors power and comparison and jealously guards the right to make policy—a prerogative his values preclude him from exercising. The ever-expanding universe of intellectual enrichment allows him independence to pursue whatever his mind is capable of grasping while balance in all things precludes the external judgments that could threaten his treasured diversity. In it all is a basis for the detachment that permits our Cartesian to be a spectator rather than an actor, a stance that supposedly assures his use of reason in all things. Such a statement is, of course, extreme. It represents the context of relationships, however, that exists to varying degrees throughout higher education. It provides an image that is useful in illuminating academic organization.

3

Organization without Structure:
The Academic Department

Placing the practicing academician into an organizational context is a study in contradictions. The cohesive force that provides the foundation for any organization is generally viewed as dedication to a collective activity. This approach offers little explanation for group response in a university. Academia's principle of integration is more accurately portrayed as dedication to collective values. Only when concepts of association are expanded beyond roles and functions to include the cultural and normative aspects of how an individual sees his ties to a system does the basis of academic organization become comprehensible.

The apparent contradiction of academia is that although faculty devotion is to larger principles, faculty loyalty is not necessarily to the larger institution of the university that appears to the outsider to shelter the principles that the academician may hold in reverence. Loyalty, in fact, is to an abstraction, to the culture that expresses academic principles. Faculty commitment is individual, and to the extent that collectivity is perceived, the faculty sees itself, rather than the university as a whole, as embodying the values and norms that provide the major ingredient for binding participants together. The dominance of the cultural and normative aspects of harmony over other features of cohesiveness (those that center attention on the function of participants) serves as the basis for the view popular among academicians that the faculty is the university. Other constituents—administrators, students, and benefactors—are excluded by the academician from this community of values.

Collegiality

When organization is collegial each member supposedly has equal power and authority with every other member. Academic organization is collegial, and outsiders sometimes suppose that collegiality occurs at the level of the full corporate faculty. But this observation misses the point of academic organization. In his classic treatment of organization, Max Weber saw collegium as having an underlying assumption. Weber set forth the proposition that prior to the existence of the corporate group, a number of autocephalous smaller groups maintained independent existence and came together when they experienced a need to reconcile the points of view of their various technical specialties. Under this genesis of organization, collegial discussion was selected as the means for achieving union.[1] As applied to academia, the smaller autocephalous groups are the discipline-oriented departments, and the act of joining together for purposes of collegial discussion formed the university. Thus collegiality initially occurs at the level of the department.

In the experience of American higher education, nothing analogous to departments predated the larger institution. In fact, most specializations found in the academic discipline represented today by a department emerged from the initial considerations of religion and philosophy, the mothers of academic discipline. Nevertheless, in their adoption of the collegial concept, academicians have clearly indicated that precedence, and whatever power they believe to be inherent to the system, should be afforded the department. Implicitly, academia employs the myth of a prior independent position for departments, a voluntary act of union in the formation of the university, and the use of corporate reciprocity to achieve whatever adjustment in interdepartmental relationships may become necessary. Barzun refers to this illusive quality of departmental kinship in his comment that relations within and among departments have no rules of order and reflect bargains of the dim past.[2] Dressel and his associates were able to verify in their survey of 1,200 faculty members that it is indeed the department which receives the basic loyalty of the academician.[3]

Much of an academician's experience confirms departmental dominance. The ways a college treats membership, recruitment, rewards, and communications all tend to support this view of a university's organization. Membership in a tenured faculty is by election, with the nomination coming from the department that makes its decision largely on the basis of the candidate's commitment to and attainment within his discipline. Recruitment by a department is conducted with a view to strengthening its professional specialization much more than to achieving broad institutional objectives. Seldom do the "liberal education credentials" of one candidate for a vacant faculty position assure selection over another who boasts professional excellence, even in an undergraduate liberal arts college.

Once membership is achieved, tangible benefits come largely through departments. As one faculty member assesses another for the purpose of apportioning the rewards of tenure and promotion, there is a tendency to fall back on something more tangible than university service, student-orientedness, or participation in general education. Administrators may press upon the college, as they did during the early 1970s, the public's demand for a relevant curriculum that deemphasizes discipline. Senior professors often claim to stand above narrow departmental loyalties. Yet, both administrators and senior faculty can become exceedingly disciplinary in judging junior academicians. The broader aspects of academic performance associated with college service and general education are considered "soft" and difficult to evaluate when compared to the so-called diamond hardness of performance within an academic discipline. Evaluators almost invariably look to the professional record in the academician's discipline in seeking the distinctions that allow one person to be promoted while another is denied this recognition. This practice is not without justification. Necessarily, the rigor in which academicians take pride is tied to their disciplines.

The communication patterns of a university are probably as important as the reward structure in sustaining the academician's proclivity for departmental dominance. Only within a department is communication assured. With the tendency for a balanced allocation of resources to achieve an all-encompassing intellectual atmosphere, and with the avoidance of interdisciplinary comparisons, communication across departmental lines is at times nonexistent. It is possible for academicians from different departments to be part of the same faculty at a relatively small college for a number of years and still not know one another unless they happen to serve together on a collegewide committee. In this phenomenon, we can still see the operational justification for the myth of the autocephalous prototype of the university.

In achieving its purpose, one department has little reason to communicate with another. When faculty members do communicate among themselves across departmental boundaries, they generally abandon departmental identification. An academician may be selected for collegewide committees on a representational basis, but in his behavior, he does not usually represent. As an independent practitioner, he speaks for himself, a tendency that usually characterizes faculty performance when an individual works beyond his department. One exception may be performance on a curriculum committee. When this device is used to assure a rational and high-quality curriculum, an academician will assume a stance of representing his department when another department wishes to introduce a course that appears to infringe upon the disciplinary prerogatives of his own unit. But even in this instance, he may be more concerned with protecting the purity of the discipline than with representing the rights of the group of which the defender is a member.

For the most part, therefore, no pattern of communication among faculty exists that corresponds to the structure of the university. In an administrative sense, messages may proceed from the individual as the basic producing unit to the department of discipline-related colleagues and on to the other parts of the university. But when communication occurs for purposes of advancing intellectual activity (the real business of the university), the academician abandons structure to communicate directly. The secondary role assigned to institutional communication may seem unusual insofar as the academician identifies basically with his discipline as depicted by the department, and it would be assumed that he would naturally communicate with other academicians through his department. But his proclivity for independent performance, combined with the symbolism of "faculty (and not departments) as university," gets in the way. The department comes close, therefore, to being excluded from those channels of communication through which an academician from one department speaks to a colleague from another. This tendency is not unreasonable. The communicators do not share the discipline of either of their respective departments. Because the department is meant to reflect discipline, it usually has no role in such communications.

Within a university there is what might be considered vertical communication between faculty and the administration. It is here that the department is critical. This business need not concern the individual faculty member on a day-to-day basis. Both Kerr and Parsons have noted a peculiarity of academic organization; that coordination between the department and managerial units of a university is pertinent principally for obtaining the resources needed by the academician to perform his mission.[4] The output of a university, whether it be instruction or research, comes close to being beyond the control of the administrator who identifies with the larger institution. The effect of such a relationship is that the individual tenured faculty member, with his near inherent right to be supported and with his freedom on matters of fashioning the product of the university, is left unencumbered by most institutional concerns. Academic practice leaves to the department the role of undertaking communication to garner resources from the administration while warding off outside constraints epitomized by the administration. Vertical communication is critical to the discipline and is conducted through the department.

This self-serving formulation of organization, which does not embody a clear concept of obligation beyond the department, remains firmly embedded in academic perceptions. One need only turn to the 1967 Majority Report of the Study Commission on University Governance at the University of California, Berkeley, to see it flourishing even in a multiversity at a time of strife and student dissent. The solution to California's problems proposed by the commission—largely a faculty body—was to reconstitute collegia and extend them to students to permit intellectually meaningful groups of faculty and students to develop curricula and programs. The commission concluded that "each small unit will require the freedom to develop the intellectual characteristics and traditions that mark a special community."[5] By implication, the troubles of Berkeley were laid at the doorstep of the bureaucratizing administrators who stood in the way of faculty and students drawing freely on institutional resources while following pursuits determined by small groups of affectively linked individuals. Such suggestions are not embodied only in wistful faculty proposals. "University Colleges" at several large universities have been constituted as small discrete units having the purpose of conducting education in a way that hopefully will allow for affective relationships.

From time to time, a small incident receives attention that vividly demonstrates the academician's perception of departmental prerogatives. Such an occurrence took place at the Harvard School of Public Health in 1978. The issue was supposedly a program matter—should the school emphasize science and medicine or should it give more attention in its instruction to the planning and managerial aspects of health programs? Several faculty wished to retain the former approach, but the dean favored shifting to the latter. The faculty accused the dean of purposely not filling four vacant positions that would assure the continuation of the school's existing program emphasis. At the same time, they charged, he was attempting to recruit faculty for four new positions that were defined to implement his own ideas. The dean's rebuttal was that a reorientation of the school's program called for a significant reallocation of funds, and because no department wanted to bear the burden of such sacrifice, he was compelled to act against the advice of certain department members. The real issue was thereupon brought into focus—an administrator was having difficulty incorporating departments into a total institutional perspective.

There was a further complication. It so happened that the dean's training was not in a public health discipline. In attempting to create a unified school from what he alluded to as a "confederation of departments," he was working to establish a single set of criteria for fund raising and for recruiting students and faculty, all of which the departments heretofore had done individually. This objective was in addition to his moves to exercise some control over the curriculum. Moreover, many of the faculty maintained that personnel decisions on retention, promotion, and tenure should be made by departmental committees constituted solely of individuals from the candidate's discipline. The dean disagreed. In the faculty's view, all difficulties stemmed from the fact that an outsider was tampering with their affairs. Finally, when the dean sought a new chairman for the nutrition department from outside the field of nutrition, the faculty concluded that he had carried his interdisciplinary approach too far.[6] At this point, they appealed to the president. Not once in this entire affair was a faculty member reported to have claimed to be personally aggrieved. All transgressions were said to be against the department and the discipline. The academic concept of collegiality had been violated.

The Purpose of Program Structure

Martin Trow and others have noted somewhat ruefully the absence of a widely shared sense of institution in academia and the resulting inability of a university to gain the loyalty of participating faculty.[7] One lament is that loyalties are so narrow that whenever an issue transcends the department, confusion and tension are likely. In a few cases, common themes have been developed at the institutional level by means of group commitment to some concept of education that cannot be served simply through departmental or disciplinary loyalties. Honors programs, preceptorials, residence learning experiences, and interdisciplinary curricula constitute notable examples. But none of these provides an organizing theme for a university or college in the same way as academic discipline.

When departmental structure and discipline are ignored in the formulation of an academic program, unusual things can happen. During the late 1960s and early 1970s, at a time of student-centered thinking, some of America's more imaginative educators elected to set aside discipline and departments and to recast education to allow the achievement of such lofty humanistic objectives as "maturing of the whole individual." An idea of the temper of the times can be obtained from the example of St. Mary's, a public college in Maryland, where the announced purpose of the institution was to "celebrate life." Particularly at the so-called innovative small colleges was the department viewed with suspicion. Often it was attacked as a parochial and wicked device for assuring that faculty interests prevailed over those of the student. Departments and their disciplines, it was charged, stood for the narrow expression of intellect over experience!

Perhaps three of the better known experimental colleges at which this view has prevailed are Santa Cruz, Evergreen, and Hampshire. These and others that were established during the 1960s had a number of common elements, mostly the setting aside of traditional academic structure found in disciplines and departments and the abandonment of accepted grading practices. In a few extreme cases, courses were discarded as units of learning. At their inception, these schools expunged certain words from their vocabulary. Notably, any reference to departments was eliminated. The term was replaced by "boards of study," "programs," "desks," "theme colleges," and a host of other organizational designators. The new institutions emphasized the features of curriculum which departments were accused of stifling. These included topically organized learning exercises, student choice, an egalitarian ethic between student and faculty, and the obfuscation of clear lines of administrative authority. Curriculum was to be problem oriented, competency based, devoted to modes of learning, or directed toward conceptual inquiry rather than for purposes of making students conversant with a body of knowledge in a discipline.[8]

Although participants in these types of institutions did not seem to realize it, they were really perpetrating in their colleges a blatant form of egocentrism. In most of them, the rate of faculty turnover was high, but a handful of founding fathers and mothers hung on and constantly looked to their own near past to revel in a claim of personal responsibility for establishing the unique features of their college, which, they claimed, were qualitatively superior to the crusty practices of the traditional school. Recruiting also supported the ego to the extent that emphasis was placed on selecting those who were imaginative and dedicated to "new ways" of learning. Little thought was given to balanced coverage of a corpus of knowledge represented by a discipline, which became secondary, along with methodology. Some of these schools even bragged that the faculty blend need not fit any particular curriculum. The guiding principles seemed to be personal choice and affective relationships. Each participant, whether student or faculty, proceeded in a self-centered little world.

These colleges were illustrative of academia insofar as they were organized around values. But they violated Bell's notion of the individual's sense of attachment to something intellectual beyond himself. The prevailing and ever-changing views of the open society had been invited into the institution at these experimental colleges to the detriment of Cartesian stability, which allows the academician time and conditions for his intellectual pursuits. Moreover, they stood on the assertion that with proper motivation (provided by caring faculty), students need not be tied to discipline, which would be replaced by a close student-faculty relationship in academic advising.

The faculties of these institutions also failed to realize (and would stoutly deny) that they were elitist in concept and organization. Their underlying assumption was that students as well as faculty brought mental discipline, an individual appreciation of methodology, intellectual deftness, and skills of expression with them—that they had already been educated. This implication did not fit with the egalitarian ethos of academicians who had set aside discipline. And when their neophytes proved not to be educated, standards suffered as students and faculty in their affective and egocentric fervor drifted further from the mental discipline of learning. In some cases, a means was found under one guise or another to reintroduce the discipline which the traditional department has represented and taught. In a way, therefore, the experimental colleges of the 1960s were also parasitic to the major body of higher education, at least to the extent that they claimed to have successfully disposed of departments and traditional disciplines even while they continued to trade upon them.

A good case study of the results of disregarding discipline is provided by Stockton State College, which was founded in the late 1960s on the premise of unspecified concepts of innovation. At this institution, faculty organized into programs rather than departments. Although these had a discipline or career bias, academicians were encouraged to seek membership in more than one program and to teach under a variety of disciplinary designators. For administrative purposes, divisions were established in the college—social science; natural science, arts and humanities, and administrative science. Rather than being traditional faculties of arts, business, and so on, comprised of strong departments, each division was a large multidisciplinary department. Divisional staffing was not limited to specified disciplines. The composition of each division was determined by how the faculty saw program needs. The Natural Science Division hired psychologists rather than call upon the Social Science Division to provide "services" from its psychology program. Management Sciences did the same with a logician.

To further deemphasize departments, students took half their courses in general education, which was touted as "another way of learning." General Studies courses were not identified with a discipline. In this portion of the curriculum, faculty were encouraged to teach material far removed from their areas of graduate training. Serendipity and even frivolity were encouraged. Under the heading of General Studies, a sociologist taught a course on wild mushrooms, a biologist took on international organization, and a business administration instructor tried his hand at expository writing. A reformed alcoholic in the business program offered a course on the influence of drink upon businessmen. A comparative literature professor engaged students in transactional analysis, while a chemistry instructor led students into sensory deprivation. The chaos reached a level where hypnotism in the classroom had to be banned. The zealotry of the situation was revealed in the expectation that all faculty members devote 40 percent of their teaching load to such courses. Those who did not, or who used the General Studies designator to disguise a straight discipline-related course, were considered misfits. Some were actually dismissed for the offense.

An incident that illuminated underlying faculty perceptions occurred when the psychologists hired by the Natural Science Division for the mathematics and biology programs experienced what they considered to be discrimination at the hands of their mathematician and biologist colleagues in promotion and tenure. Immediately they sought transfers to the Social Science Division, where they could identify with the psychology program and have their performance as psychologists evaluated more equitably. There was clearly a difference between the college's rhetoric about interdisciplinary programs and the implicit views of faculty. The amusing aspect of the entire affair was that those who practiced this discrimination were staunch advocates of the college's disregard for discipline and department in its organization.

Generally, such efforts at so-called interdisciplinary education require the individual academician to set aside the sustaining ties which his discipline provides with the intellectual world beyond his college. It is a first step toward the loss of true intellectual excitement. Some advocates of interdisciplinary pursuits forget that before a program can be interdisciplinary, discipline must be mastered. What they usually mean by "interdisciplinary" is the presentation of material in a way that is without a profound organizing theme. It involves courses that provide no opportunity for confronting methodological issues. Popular topics take precedence over the scholarly approach of attempting to discern levels of generalization which establish control over and continuity for discipline-oriented material and therefore a context for explaining social, artistic, or scientific phenomena.

Within a topically organized program, teaching cannot always be related to the academician's research, and an important element of unity is lost in his work. His role becomes that of another learner who has only a little more to offer in classroom discussion than a good student. The classic concept of a teacher imparting knowledge and encouraging students in pursuit of intellect is transformed into that of a group organizer and facilitator. When one college attempted to organize an interdisciplinary program of study around the theme "Humanities' Perspectives on Technology," a faculty participant was prompted to remark, "The definition of a true professor has always been that he knows his boundaries and has a strong sense of territoriality. He can argue that every step outside the strict traditions of his discipline is at the expense of professional excellence."[9]

From outside the academician's own university the links of discipline are reinforced by professional journals, professional organizations (and the meetings they sponsor), and cooperation in research with disciplinary colleagues at distant universities. Herein lie important elements of the sense of belonging, the reward structure, and the communication channels perceived by the academician. Administrative decisions that deemphasize the department are not likely to affect this network. Academic disciplines represent the way knowledge is used in our society. They meet the requirements of industry and government for both research and trained manpower; they sustain not only the academician's ties to intellect but also the very intellectual life of our country. Objections to departments and disciplines are raised only among those having romantic notions about the personal experience of learning at the undergraduate level as opposed to the institutional processes of educating and of applying knowledge for all purposes.

The incongruities that arise from deemphasis of discipline are much the same as when politically activist students during the 1960s called upon faculty to join them in radical causes and to convert the university from a place of intellectual inquiry into a center for political advocacy. In such instances, the academician is being asked to abandon the structures and processes that give his endeavors meaning. If he responds to the call, he must extend an open invitation to students to consume as they see fit his most valuable commodity—the time he would otherwise devote to scholarly pursuits. In interdisciplinary or socially oriented programs, little attention is given to the condition that brought many faculty into the academy in the first place, namely, an inclination for an independent profession that removes those controls over the use of one's time that are imposed in bureaucratic organization. At the heart of the academic endeavor are the Cartesian principles of independence. Departmental structure and academic discipline are seen by most academicians as serving to protect these values. In the final analysis, inter- or nondisciplinary pursuits can only lead to greater institutional commitment—an obligation that most academicians are loath to accept.

Difficulty usually occurs in sustaining faculty enthusiasm for any teaching assignment that is extraneous to departmental offerings. It is an old story at most colleges and universities that support for a general education program tends to erode over time. At the outset, the commitment to deemphasize discipline by teaching in a program that is only for general education purposes may be solemnly accepted by many faculty. But before long, the task of convincing individual academicians to offer such courses can create as much tension as anything experienced in the life of a college. An exception can be found in cases where a general education core program has a strong disciplinary bias, where specific courses in the program are taught exclusively by members of separate departments, and possibly where each such course is required of all students. At this point, general education can become the bread and butter of a department that happens to have few majors. It is a means of introducing students to a discipline, and it amounts to little more than a distribution device within the curriculum. It assures all faculty an equitable portion of enrollments and thereby enhances institutional stability.

The Department as a Small Group

Going beyond the meaning, rewards, and purposes that are assigned to the department and its discipline, small group theory also provides insight into the operations of academic departments. This approach is useful for explaining (1) how an academician relates to group goals, (2) the phenomenon of self-oriented behavior, (3) the idea of self-interest, (4) the academic perception of security, and (5) the place of power and sanctions within the academic structure.

Small group analysis rests on the assumption that the behavior of individuals operating in groups has characteristics derived as much from the effect of face-to-face interaction as from the functions of the organization in which these individuals work. Even at large universities where the membership of a single department exceeds the size of an entire faculty at a small school, there is an inclination among faculty to draw together into small groups in which the affective aspects of community are emphasized. One such dimension of grouping at the large university is the senior members of a department, who may informally hold joint responsibility for making the department's more important decisions. Alternatively, departmental committees permit the playing out of small group relationships. Individual faculty members belong to one of a set of committees, or to an area within the discipline. Each has a scope of activity that is limited to specified portions of the department's full range of responsibility.[10] We have already noted the inclination at Berkeley in 1967 of faculty and students to organize themselves in "small units" having the "freedom to develop the intellectual characteristics and traditions that mark a special community."[11]

Sidney Verba's survey of political behavior establishes several characteristics of the small group. His findings indicate that insofar as group membership is important to participants, there will be pressure for accord. The decision-making process of small groups is fashioned to prevent conflict from coming to the surface. Voting and the divisions this action manifests may be avoided. Instead, a consensus is permitted to emerge. Any consensus that is established under these conditions does not imply agreement on all matters coming before the group. Rather, it is indicative of a sense of group solidarity in the face of outside forces that are viewed as not always congenial. The desire for harmony and protection outweighs the importance of differences that arise among members of the group. Group influence may be instrumental both in shaping a participant's general attitudes about his endeavors and in determining his conclusions regarding any specific issue the group may confront.[12]

These relationships described by Verba correspond to the behavior patterns in most academic departments. They reinforce the Cartesian stability which the academician finds so necessary for his work. Small group practices do not, however, depict attitudes at the level of the corporate faculty where the size of the body and a less compelling sense of cohesiveness do not allow for Verba's conditions. Meetings of the corporate faculty may be torn by strife over an educational issue. But at the level of the department it can be a different story. Many of the individuals who are most vociferous in pressing debate against a proposal when considered by the corporate faculty will now accept it.

At least outwardly, individual preference fades in the presence of departmental considerations. This premise does not mean that all is sweetness and light within the department. Backbiting and pettiness are sometimes so pronounced that they are difficult to believe. But the condition does suggest that within the total organizational structure of a university, department members see value in keeping outsiders far removed from whatever conflict occurs within their ranks. Very seldom is a dean, for example, invited to mediate a departmental dispute. In fact, this sense of exclusivity will tend to mitigate differences. In one case, a dean insisted on taking a hand in ending internecine warfare within a music department after students were drawn into the vituperation over who would be the next chairman. The situation was quickly calmed when department members were told that the associate dean (whose discipline was English literature) would serve as acting chairman for a period. Miraculously, the dispute was resolved. An atmosphere of guarded camaraderie developed between the contending factions and even between their candidates.

Group Goals

The nature of the department is revealed through an examination of how academia relates to a group goal. In the academic institutional setting, group goals are almost always secondary to individual goals. Because an academician pursues both teaching and research independently, group goals can only be enabling. They generally pertain to some aspect of an institution's configurations which facilitates the achievement of individual goals. Acquiring more research funds, liberalizing sabbatical policies, and establishing lighter teaching loads would be good examples of academic group goals.

Social psychologists maintain that the achievement of group goals is furthered by people working in proximity to one another. Apparently, an assortment of social motives which become relevant for an individual working in the presence of others is not evoked when a person works alone.[13] The style of academic performance provides little opportunity for working together. Consequently, it does not evoke the motives that contribute to strong faculty group goals.

Regarding the research aspects of an academician's performance, intellectual activity may be stimulated as the result of academicians working together in a university setting, but does it lead to the formulation and achievement of group goals? Research centers, industrial research operations, and nonprofit "think tanks" have adapted their intellectual activities to collective goals. But their approach contradicts the Cartesian prescription that truths are more likely to be found by one man than by a whole people. The term "independent," as applied to an academician's research, does not always carry the connotation of solitary activity. It does, however, mean that no one other than the participant determines the scope and content of activity, which is constantly subject to individual reinterpretation. Each academician insists on pursuing research of his choice. Here we see how the industrial research specialist who operates within the context of a group goal differs from the academician who does not.

Academicians do cooperate with one another, but by and large they have resorted to a means for participating in joint ventures that does not violate their norms of individual and holistic performances. A common objective sometimes binds together scholars who share data as one builds on another's efforts in working individually toward the resolution of a single problem. There is also collaborative research in multiauthored publications. In the case of the latter, chapters are usually prepared by and identified with individual writers. Performance is segmented rather than differentiated. Cooperation takes place; a common theme is developed; but the individual's identity is never lost within a group.

For complex research tasks requiring organization and sustained activity, a more intricate device is used to facilitate cooperative efforts among academicians. This is the specialized institute, often controlled by one or two major faculty figures who employ others (including a number of nonteaching professionals) as research collaborators. Those who have been associated with such an enterprise readily admit that it can put a great strain on professional relationships. The important point for our discussion is that the institute provides an alternative to collaborating within a department. Consequently, it relieves the department of the tensions involved when one academician works under the direction of another.

A research institute's nonteaching professionals usually have terminal degrees, but often these individuals are not in the tenure track of the university at which they happen to be located. They do not qualify as academicians. They are external to the collegium, and the usual faculty sensitivities over the ascriptive and independent nature of a participant's position do not apply to them. Institutes allow for cooperation and communication across disciplinary lines without the necessity for observing all the attributes of the academic political culture. In an institute, research collaborators are not necessarily permitted to determine the nature of their own work; the scarcity of resources can be acknowledged; allocations among disciplines need not be balanced; and the individual can be held accountable for how he spends his time. Organization can be authoritative, and interdisciplinary comparisons can be made. Without tainting the norms of academic organization or political process embodied in the department, academicians working in an institute can organize themselves to accommodate the standards of our pluralistic society.

Self-Oriented Behavior

In most types of organization, consensus generally pertains both to the substance of group goals and to the chosen means of pursuing these goals. Academicians bear neither constraint. Independent, holistic, and ascriptive performance is necessarily self-oriented. The work of John W. Thibaut and Harold H. Kelley suggests that "groups showing a high incidence of self-oriented behavior have been found to express less satisfaction with their meetings and their decisions, to perceive themselves as less unified, and to meet for longer periods while completing fewer agenda items."[14] Anyone who has been exposed to the faculty group process is compelled to agree that the foregoing is an accurate description of the academic phenomenon. Self-oriented behavior is a condition that precludes the degree of compliance necessary to constitute and achieve group goals.

David Riesman points out that in cases where a faculty sees its institution as having achieved recognition as a model for higher education, its members can rise above self-oriented behavior. Intense loyalty to the institution and its program can develop.[15] When this condition occurs, group goals may operate at both the departmental and institutional levels. Whereas pursuit of personal recognition through individual activities is the norm in academia, acquiring this quality through group performance apparently becomes satisfying only if the academician is permitted to enjoy, but is not called upon to develop, the conditions that facilitate group esteem. To require the commitment on his part that is necessary for developing group esteem would place an unnatural constraint on his use of time. From the standpoint of faculty, institutional prestige "happens"; it is not something they will work to create.

A well-established aspect of institutional behavior is that group goals require group choices. To adopt and then to attain goals means that individual perceptions must be sacrificed to those of the group. It has already been pointed out that academicians disdain choices of this nature. Their appreciation of activity is that it should be ever-growing and all-encompassing to the limits of whatever knowledge the mind is capable of grasping. Accepting group choices introduces a limiting factor by giving one set of activities preference over another. In an academic setting, difficulty is likely to arise in gaining faculty acceptance of the choices implicit in far-reaching collective goals. The goals that are accepted will be vague and open to both individual interpretation and varying degrees of adherence. This academic perception is one reason why program budgeting techniques with their goal-setting purposes cannot be expected to operate within the university as they do in industry or government.

Self-Interest

Perhaps one of the more subtle aspects of an academician's association with the department is the way he sees personal interest being realized through group relationships. In our pluralistic society, the individual's view of his place of employment is generally tied to plus and minus calculations associated with personal gain. Group membership and loyalty are justified by the rewards that the participant realizes from affiliation. Material sacrifice by the individual for the sake of the employing institution is made only with the understanding that this act will preserve employment (and the income to be derived from it) or will enhance income and position at a later date. The relationship is essentially monetary and contractual.

This approach is not applicable in the academic setting insofar as academicians are not motivated by the same well-defined acquisitive concerns that are found in our open society. Within the university, relationships tend to reflect a relatively low level of individual interest. This outlook is based on the intrinsic qualities that are attributed to academic discipline. Many faculty have difficulty distinguishing between the benefits derived from resources being used for the academic program within their discipline and those allowed for salary increases. It is bewildering for the outsider to encounter the academician who would make a salary increase secondary to funds in support of his curriculum. But a certain logic is present. This attitude incorporates the meaning of professing.

The collective bargaining agreements of faculty unions demonstrate this point. In other occupations, collective bargaining is about compensation—salary and leisure. Fringe benefits loom large. Liberal retirement, health programs, and safety features associated with work usually constitute the body of these contracts. In the case of faculty unions, it is almost impossible to stop here. The size of incremental pay increases can at times be all but ignored in the bargaining over other matters. Union representatives will ask that goals be set for travel funds to allow faculty to attend more professional meetings; all types of schemes that support individual professional activity will find their way into contracts. Faculty will even attempt to set budget allocations for acquisitions of the college library. Management can sometimes extract as much at the bargaining table by agreeing to organize and finance an autonomous research institute in which faculty have a dominant voice as by giving additional percentage points in across-the-board pay increases.

The same academician who sets such unusual priorities for himself may be quick to question allocations, however, if the issue is between faculty salaries and university expenditures for strengthening the overall institution through improved administration, better alumni relations, more intercollegiate sports, or possibly additional student aid. Even then, the criticism of such expenditures is not expressed as institutional well-being versus the personal interests of faculty members. Rather, academic programs, as expressed through the disciplines, are pictured as suffering at the hands of the university. It is not uncommon for agitated faculty members to make representations to a board of trustees or to censure a president for failure to allocate funds so as to embellish the educational mission of the college.

This is not to say that faculty never show interest in salary increases. The important point is how they show interest. A common formulation is the argument that an increase in salary for faculty is an investment of the type that is best calculated to improve the college's educational offerings. The same argument is used to justify the establishing of a well-endowed chair. Program benefit is in the forefront of argumentation rather than the personal benefit of the individual who will receive more money. If pressed to defend his rationale, the academician may contend that to the extent he can be relieved from the burden of maintaining himself, he can devote more time to his work with advantage accruing to the program. The academician's sense of the material is interpreted from the standpoint of the meaning to which resources will be devoted—the pursuit of knowledge—and not from that of personal comfort. The idea of comfort is approached in other ways, such as unrestricted time and the conditions that sustain the stability of the Cartesian environment.

A philosophical basis for the preference sometimes given program over personal interests is provided by John Dewey's suggestion that educators systematically depreciate "interest" because of a difference they perceive between emotion and intellect. The image of emotion is personal advantage and friction arising from competition; the image of intellect is that of capturing truth.[16] For the academician, of course, the latter is identified with his discipline. As in the observation adapted from Daniel Bell, the academician, in his concern with scholarship, learning, books, ideas, and the past, centers his attention on things beyond himself.

It sometimes seems unusual to an outsider that the academician, who is dedicated to the individual mode of performance, will make personal interest a secondary consideration. The key, of course, is that the academician's position derives its legitimacy from ascription provided by his achievement in a specified discipline. Thus the discipline becomes a more important source of identity than the goods and material well-being that support prestige in our pluralistic society and that the general public associates with self-interest.

Security

Security is an important aspect of all organization, and in this regard academia is no exception. Within the complex set of relationships found in a university, it is natural for the academician to find security in the small group ties of the department. Small group theory suggests that group cohesiveness results from the group serving as a reference point for its members in determining social reality.[17] As a corollary, loyalty develops when security becomes associated in the minds of its members with a group's status. Certainly, the department is a major point of social reality for the academician. His personal commitment to the values of higher education is interpreted as an academic discipline expressed through a department. The process of academic integration, the nature of collegiality, and the means of dispensing rewards all reflect the reality of the department. Except for a limited number of well-known scholars, an academician's worth is often assessed by the caliber of the department with which he is associated.

We have already noted the problems created for the academic culture by nondisciplinary programs. One reason faculty avoid them is that they provide only a marginal identity for the participant—a condition that makes the professoriate insecure. In teaching outside his field, the academician, according to David Riesman, is confronted with the normative concern of causing alien material of another discipline to lose its "technical virtuosity."[18] Riesman is himself an academician, and his formulation reflects the academic perspective. It amply demonstrates academia's perception of the individual's relationship to his discipline and therefore to his department. It involves an individual's values, and to this extent it also has a powerful influence on his sense of security.

The work of Dressel and his associates indicates that the context in which an academician works varies with seniority. The promotion from assistant, to associate, and finally to full professor is accompanied by a shift in viewpoint regarding both reference group and ideas of security. A progression is involved, which first emphasizes the discipline, then the department as an end in itself, and finally, in some cases, the university.[19] The assistant professor, perhaps not yet having tenure, does not identify totally with the group. He may still cling to the hope of becoming a scholar who is widely recognized throughout the discipline. Lacking tenure, if he has security at all it is to be found in the discipline. The full professor, at the other extreme, may have assumed the local prestige that allows him some influence at the university level, and he experiences secure feelings in the exercise of this influence. In the middle range is the associate professor, who has neither the cosmopolitan view of the assistant nor the institutional outlook of the full professor. He has achieved sufficient stature for his efforts at departmental politics to show results. His experience tells him that the possibility of lateral movement to other institutions is decreasing. He faces the prospect of remaining in the same position for a number of years. Dressel's findings, therefore, fit well with the vision of the man in the middle. For him there is indeed little difference between personal interests and the group prerogatives of the department. And there should be no surprise that he finds security in the department.

Usually the security that is provided by a department operates in a passive manner, being in the background and serving as a foundation that gives the academician the confidence to act. It is no wonder that from this perspective alone, most academicians remain close to their disciplines. If an academician who finds himself extended and beyond his discipline perceives a personal threat of a professional nature, he will withdraw into the protection of the department. This practice is followed in a great number of the confrontations with the college administration. Because chairmen are the point of contact with the administration, they are often at the center of such confrontations. At such times it is difficult to determine when a dispute is with the chairman personally and when it involves an issue that truly exercises most of the department. Department members usually close ranks around the colleague who is contending. Whatever the origins of the dispute, it ends as a classic case between faculty portrayed as department and the administration portrayed as the bureaucracy. In one such instance, a chairman turned up at the dean's office with his entire department for what was supposed to have been a personal discussion of an issue that only concerned the two individuals. An academician who cannot solicit this kind of support from colleagues in times of difficulty has few defenses other than claims of racial or sexual bias (as these may apply) or violation of his rights under a collective bargaining contract if one exists. Otherwise, there is only the lonely bitterness that an academic career can carry for the independent and entrepreneurial practitioner who may have been bettered in a contest with the administration.

Power and Sanctions

At the heart of any organization's approach to appropriate relations among its members is the place of power. Indeed, the academician's concept of authority has a major influence in shaping the institution in which he works. Having ensconced himself in a disciplinary department, it might be supposed that the academician would develop this entity as a bastion of strength for advancing discipline-related claims. But the academician does not require organizational authority to achieve his mission. Personal prestige and organizational support will suffice. Authority in any guise is a threat. If faculty, as a group, attempt to garner power in a university, they do so generally only to dissipate it so that it cannot be used against them as individuals. Herein lies one of the purposes of vesting authority in an academic committee. This same perception of authority at the level of the university applies to the department. It is not meant to have authority. It only protects the individual from outside forces, principally through symbolic devices such as pronouncements concerning the inviolable nature of department prerogatives. Nor has power a place in relations among departments. These are to be guided by corporate reciprocity in which administrators of the college are supposed to do little more than maintain the balance among constituent units.

The exercise of organizational power in business and government depends on structure, that is, a hierarchy with distinctions among individual members which assure that all functions furthering group interests receive due attention, leadership to give persistence and direction to group efforts, and sanctions to discipline the errant. This model is, of course, the antithesis of the academic perception. A department avoids hierarchy. Other than special committee assignments and acknowledgment of teaching and research specialties, there is no distinction among department members. In functions, the instructor does (and is expected to do) exactly the same things as a full professor. The horizontal equivalence of organization found in the department allows for none of the specialized roles that make a group effective. In their place, each member has maximum freedom to pursue individual preferences at his own pace. This structure limits the capability of the group when it must engage in political contests with

other groups. Mobilizing departmental faculty for any struggle is difficult. A department is not organized for bureaucratic combat.

Strong organizational leadership also stands in opposition to self-
regulated holistic performance. As a result, leadership, which in a
department is present in the office of chairman, is suspect. A department chairman often has little authority over and only limited additional prestige among colleagues. The duty of the chairman is usually
seen as helping the department to fulfill its responsibilities by facilitating the decisions taken by the membership. The position is placed in
perspective with the idea of the chairman being the normal channel of
communications with administrative or institutional level units of the
college. Seldom are the prerogatives of the chair well defined. The
chairman is clearly meant to be the creature of the department, and
the individual department member is left to manage his own affairs.
The office is viewed as so heavy a burden that at times it is difficult to
fill. Thus a chairmanship may be rotated among tenured members of
the group, vested regularly in the most junior full professor, or held by
an associate professor—the man in the middle—while senior colleagues pursue individual research, professional activities, or institutional politics.

There are, of course, colleges and universities at which a few impe-
rial chairmen still hold forth. They assign courses, determine the
schedule, distribute departmental budget allocations, make final selec-
tions in recruiting new department members, and evaluate faculty. The
tendency is, however, to assign many of these duties to committees in
which the academician's high sense of equity, his preference for balance in allocating resources, and his insistence on allowing for individual freedom can all come into play. A turning point in academic
organization probably occurred during the turmoil of the late 1960s
when many young faculty were sufficiently emboldened by the
egalitarian ethic of the day to speak out against senior colleagues. As
often as not the response was not punitive action but dismay. Thereafter, more departmental work was performed by committees.

Despite the academician's predilection to place limitations upon the
chairmanship, many still covet the position. Its importance stems from
a naive perception of how authority is exercised in an organization.
The insistence of the academician in thinking and talking about organizational power sets him apart from individuals engaged in industry or
government. In these cases, the term that is consistently used is
responsibility, referring to organization attributes of a position,

whoever the incumbent. A dispassionate or perhaps once-removed quality is present in institutional responsibility which the academician, with his highly individualized view of the world, cannot always grasp. In his politics, he sees power as having a personal aspect.

This interpretion of power determines how the academician views the authority of others and is a key to his resentment when authority is exercised over him. But in addition, it often governs his use of authority when he is vested with an administrator's responsibilities. The thought of becoming chairman, in fact, is approached by many academicians quixotically, with little thought of the duties that might be involved. The value of the position is seen as being in the title, as if it were only honorific. A chairman often does not consider group goals in his actions; he thinks only of the discretion the position allows him. By personally exercising the limited budgetary authority available to a department, a chairman will sometimes attempt to release himself in small ways from dependence on the university, a relationship with which the academician lives uncomfortably. Thus, departmental allocations may be devoted heavily to the chairman's specialty within the discipline. Because he sees power in personal terms, this action somehow seems legitimate. Some chairmen are also prone to a popular management technique that reveals an untutored view of administration—they attempt to conceal actions from colleagues. This approach is often possible because of the absence of regular channels of communication among faculty on administrative matters.

Even when a chairman does not behave in this fashion, many department members suspect that he does. This is one of the more common complaints against those holding the position. Any action taken by the chairmen without assiduous consultation in the department may ultimately be viewed as capricious and arbitrary by his colleagues and is likely to become a source of friction. If there is a time when tensions come to the surface within a department, it is upon the election or reelection of a chairman. Old grievances are then aired. The issue often is not who will be chairman in the future but involves a recitation of the perceived transgressions of the chairman in the past. In some cases, after the exercise is completed, the existing chairman will be reelected by those who expressed the most vociferous objections to his conduct!

An additional perspective of power in a department can be obtained by considering sanctions, that is, group response to an act that violates a shared idea regarding the norms of conduct. If power is considered the medium for controlling action, then it must be complemented by some means of achieving that purpose. In any situation, the issue is: What consequence does an actor face if he makes known an intention not to fulfill a task which his peers consider an obligation?

Small group theory maintains that in situations where membership is important to the individual, few penalties will be necessary.[20] Consensus building and acquiescence of potentially divergent elements will supposedly prevail. But there is an underlying implication attached to this formulation that threatens the efficacy of consensus itself. When a consensual approach to operations becomes a norm of an organization, it can preclude the application of sanctions against individuals who deviate from a group's standards. The necessity for sanctions within an organization only emphasizes the absence of consensus. It means that competing ideas about norms of conduct are present. This very admission is destructive to the atmosphere of harmony upon which the academician depends for stability in the cherished Cartesian environment. Academicians, therefore, often prefer to ignore infractions by a colleague rather than impose sanctions that are ruinous to their perception of social reality.

Under stable conditions, the positive formulation of our proposition may prevail—the consensus-building norm will preclude the necessity for many sanctions. When infractions do occur they can be treated as isolated incidents of aberrant behavior and the group has no trouble meting out punishment. But in recent years the academic culture has eroded by pressure from society to accommodate the public's perceptions of training as education and external management as academic leadership. Under this assault, respect for academic group norms has become less important to the academician, possibly because today's managers have less regard for academic pretensions. The quality of community is weakened. There is less affinity for colleagues. The errant academician can sometimes ignore that his behavior is contrary to his department's expectations while supposing that he is only transgressing against an alien institution, system, or its administrators.

Even when actions of an individual member of the collegium violate the Cartesian principles, colleagues cannot allow the group to dominate the individual. Personal independence is seen as the last bastion of the profession. During periods of change or instability, there are occasions when the disciplining of a recalcitrant faculty member by the group does not occur at the department level, although juniors may occasionally be "eldered." At the same time, a certain sanctity still surrounds a department because it embodies the academician's discipline. Consequently, attempts by outsiders to impose punishment on a department member may be resisted, even by colleagues within the department who consider the offender objectionable.

The possibility of not having an annual contract renewed or not being granted tenure does exist as a sanction against those junior colleagues who do not meet standards of colleagueship. But this device is also used when young faculty are deficient in scholarship or teaching ability. It is not simply a sanction for violating group norms. Thus, the reason a university has for not renewing a contract of a faculty member may not always be clear.

The very circumstance of posing disassociation from the group as one of the institution's few discernible sanctions, and then only for academicians who are still candidates for full membership as exemplified by tenure, indicates that sanctions are not accepted as a legitimate feature of authority in the regulation of the day-to-day life of the corporate faculty. In other types of organizations, there is the option of imposing punishment while continuing the association between the offender and the institution, but for the academician this recourse seldom exists. To accept such a possibility would pose a threat to academic autonomy.

4

Equations of Power:

The Academician and the University

Beyond the security which academicians establish in their departments are the other constituencies of the university—students, administrators, and alumni. These groups stand between the academician and the public represented by the outside manager. Each can be used as a buffer for filtering out the less desirable interactions with the public. But each group also has its particular point of view, its own vision of the academy. Interplay among these visions produces the totality of the university.

The independence demanded by academicians from the university as a whole imposes upon them the necessity to maintain a distinct set of relationships with each of the other constituencies. These relations are not always characterized by the controlled intrainstitutional competition that exists in industry or government. Usually they embody less compatibility. Approaching the university from different perspectives, the constituencies can literally be working for different objectives. While the academician labors to preserve his time, students concentrate on consuming it. Administrators would control it. The difference is over what the academic endeavor really entails. Does the university produce manpower and serve the community directly as the administrator would have it? Does it enhance the personal qualities of the student receiving the education? Or is its purpose to provide an opportunity for the Cartesian practitioner to pursue whatever his mind is capable of grasping while students and the general public benefit from the by-products of the process?

A mystifying aspect of academia for the observing public is its antipathies. Many academicians dislike students because they are students. Some of this sentiment may derive from the academician's perception of student disinterest toward his discipline, a perfectly normal condition insofar as the student has not taken the vows of profession. Yet, a lack of tolerance often exists. It is not unknown for a college teacher to experience considerable anxiety over the daily classroom confrontation with students. The brusk putdown of which students accuse some instructors is often the signal of this lack of satisfaction with the teaching portion of the academic pursuit.

Similarly, some faculty and administrators dislike the other genre simply because of the role each plays. Academicians often scorn administrators' legitimacy. In the absence of an overbearing authority in the hands of either side, not even the issue of ultimate institutional objective can be resolved. Perhaps it is necessary to return to the old-fashioned labor-capital dichotomy of the earlier half of the century to find anything comparable to the contrariness that can characterize the relationships of groups participating in the common business of a university. The attitudes are doubly preplexing because every academician was at one time a student, and virtually every administrator was once a faculty member. Certainly, all are or will become alumni. Here we will examine the forces that are at work in only one of these relationships—that between the academician and the portion of the university which is viewed as the administration.

Different Outlooks—Shared Endeavors

It is a mistake to identify the administrator who works inside the university with the manager who operates from outside its walls. Rather than always representing the public's penchant for accountability, the inside administrator often intercedes to mediate on behalf of the university as a discrete entity. Private institutions are known for their independence, but in publicly financed institutions as well, the administrators—deans, vice-presidents, and president—can bitterly resent outside interference, particularly the requirements that serve a state "system" into which they might have been pressed and that cause the university to lose its identity. In this situation, the administrator tends to lose his identity as well.

If the university's administrator sees his purpose as being different from that of the system's manager, it is probably because he sees the proper function of the academy differently. The perspective of the administrator is usually more comprehensive than that of the outside manager. Rather than approaching the university as an array of individual programs for students to select as consumers, the administrator perhaps considers the intellectuality of the multidisciplinary experience embodied in the university's programs as a whole—the spirit to be found in a place of learning. The institution has meaning for him that supersedes whatever may be concluded from adding together its various parts. One example of the difference between the administrator and the manager was the case of the executive director of a state college system who could not see why the alumni of his constituent colleges could not be "systematized" into a single organization that would be more effective than the smaller independent single-college alumni groups in pressuring the state legislature. Administrators, who identify with the individual colleges, had no difficulty understanding the problems of getting alumni to work for and show loyalty to the system. The same difference occurs when managers who are serving as state regents or boards of higher education attempt, in the name of efficiency, to delete a discipline or department from a public college or block the addition of a new program at a private institution because that specialty is handled by a nearby institution. For the administrator who works from within, such a rationale violates the very idea of the university.

All boards of trustees at public institutions are not bent, of course, on serving as an arm of the state government to control public colleges and universities. Nor are all boards of private institutions benevolent and understanding of the academic enterprise while taking their lead from the university's president. In the case of the former, some boards intercede on behalf of the university and even lobby in state legislatures to forestall extraneous decisions that would limit the institution's autonomy. At private institutions, a rambunctious alumni association can cause every bit as much grief for a president as a suspicious state commissioner who attempts to manage the daily affairs of a public institution.

The accusation of interference is not just leveled against those who are associated with a university but happen to operate from beyond its administration. A university's president or vice-president can carry a rigid institutional view rather than a liberal perception of the educational process embodied in students and faculty confronting intellectual issues in discipline-related material. While warding off the intercessions of outside managers, he may attempt to subject the academic department to controls that its members see as external interference. The administrator sometimes wants departmental operations to conform to the will of the university much as the outside manager wants the university to conform to the system.

Administrators often isolate themselves from the academician by showing only marginal concern for education. At times, it is not possible to determine from the records of their meetings whether administrators are organized to further intellect or to manufacture snow tires. At a typical meeting, academic deans can devote long hours to a campus electric power failure, a squabble with the faculty union over summer salaries, complaints by the space officer that converting classrooms into specialized function rooms adds to his difficulties in scheduling regular classes, an admonishment from the business office over timely submission of student-help pay cards, anguish from the vice-president regarding the president's procrastination in naming a new dean of the business school, and outrage expressed by all the deans in response to a resolution from the board of trustees establishing new procedures for program approval. One such session finally ended with a dirty joke. The serious problems of education faced by this college were never addressed in what amounted to the monthly meeting of those who purported to provide leadership for academicians. Even more horrifying is the confession of some chairmen that department meetings of the academicians themselves are no better.

The literature on higher education devotes a great deal of attention to describing how academicians interact with administrators. The academician sees problems that arise as issues of governance, a term that has come to be used to differentiate roles within the politics of collegial organization. The principal features revealed by this literature are that the administrator has a preferred position even though his authority is highly qualified. Administrative considerations dominate on matters of budget, institutional planning, and the general affairs of the college; faculty have the prevailing voice in curriculum, faculty appointments and status, and the selection of department heads.

The ideal, of course, is that authority will be shared between the two on all these issues, particularly the authority that would otherwise be relegated to the administrator. The idea of shared governance is predicated on full disclosure of information about the affairs of the college, continuous consultation of faculty by administrators, clear procedures for decision making, time for all constituencies to react to any proposal that might be put forth, and adjustment of the positions of the various constituencies after the views of all have become known.[1] These ideas are embodied in a "Statement on Government of Colleges and Universities" devised jointly in 1966 by the American Association of University Professors, the American Council on Education, and the Association of Governing Boards.[2]

Such statements are characterized above all else by so much general language and so many indirections that it is difficult to determine where authority is to be found under the various formulas for shared governance. The conclusion to be reached from reviewing the literature and reading the statement on governance is that administrators are expected to be acutely aware of faculty sensitivities and should act against faculty advice only under the most exceptional circumstances. Shared governance is, in fact, an invitation for administrators to avoid the exercise of institutional responsibility.

This view of a university's internal relationships may seem bewildering, but the situation is not as bad as it appears. Confusion over the peculiar organizing principles of academia is created by the mind-set of our society. Modern social practice requires that all things be managed. This view satisfies a desire for efficiency that originates in the essential frugality of the American tradition. It fits our perception of society being organized for purposes of production. A specific view of management and its dominant role within an organization naturally flows from this assumption. But do the so-called basic principles of good administration which we derive from industry or even from our bureaucratic agencies apply to all organizations?

The academician considers the faculty to be the heart of the academy. Functionally, the observation is accurate. Instruction and research performed by faculty stand at the center of the institution's purpose. If we use the idea of production as an analogy, a university can be likened to an industry marketing products—instruction and research—which are offered on commercial terms to the public. There is, of course, a need for administrators to organize and direct the procedures necessary to generate the academic product. But here a fundamental characteristic of academia cannot be ignored. In Chapter 3, in our consideration of communications between faculty ensconced in their departments and administrators working in the bureaucratized portions of a university, it was observed that a curious division of labor exists between the two groups. Administrators concern themselves with the inputs from which the educational experience is fashioned, but they have little to do with output or the product itself. Faculty, who are largely self-regulated (once resources are made available), control output. Might one not assume, therefore, that with only half the mission of administrators in industry, the coordinators of academia can rightfully claim only half the authority? Is not academia a system that lends itself to liberal management balanced by the inventiveness, entrepreneurship, and quasi-administration of the academician? In this equation we can find the subtleties of governance.

Various factors influence the equations of power between the academician and the administrator. These begin with how the two groups perceive their institutional setting and how they see the world of the other. The administrator is inclined to approach the managerial offices of a university as an enterprise in which the importance of collective endeavors outweighs consideration for the individual. Administrative concerns are largely instrumental. The administrator strives for predictability in performance, which implies an effort to establish a sense of cued response throughout the organization. He attempts to impose upon his staff the supervision that brings to operations a pattern of coordinated behavior. Those who participate in the management and housekeeping of the university work toward an optimal return from whatever resources (both human and material) are available to them.

The administrator's experience is not just within the university. The purview of his concerns constitutes a world of complex relationships involving such outside groups as trustees, benefactors, alumni, state bureaucrats and legislators, federal officials, and the general public. In the late 1960s the administration at Columbia University found that it even had to consider the neighbors when it attempted to initiate a building program that would have displaced nearby residents. The important point about the administrator's position and perception is that they afford him power over the university's operations. He rests his claim to authority on a special knowledge of the institution's needs, on influence derived from his association with external constituencies, and on adherence to the art of the possible.

Although the administrator's activities may be of great concern to faculty and usually occur with faculty acquiescence, the administrative process does not always allow for faculty initiative. The administrator can easily slip into the notion that faculty, like accountants and maintenance men, are a means for achieving the university's ends. In the abstract institutional world of the administrator, the research and educational product of the university can somehow be disassociated from the individual academician who produces them. Faculty achievements are depicted to the public as the work of the institution itself. Performance is in the name of the university. Except for the most eminent of scholars, the faculty's identity tends to be lost. At this point, the academician sees the instrumental concerns of the administrator as self-serving. From the academician's perspective they amount to little more than a device for strengthening the administrator's hold over the academic endeavor.

Whereas the organizational practices of our society permit the administrator's perception to be viewed as highly desirable both by the public and by outside managers, from the standpoint of the academician holding the ethos of the faculty-dominated collegium, it can be absolutely abhorrent. The academician sees a much greater concentration of power in the administrator's activities than presidents, vice-presidents, deans, and business directors can themselves discern. If we recall the myth of autocephalous union that is implicit to collegial organization, and if we combine this idea with the academician's desire to enhance personal creativity by pursuing the knowledge of everything his mind is capable of grasping, we soon arrive at the contraints that institutional concepts can impose upon the entrepreneurial academic spirit. The effectiveness for which the administrator strives has little meaning to the academician whose view is quite different from that of his administrative colleagues.

Within the faculty, little can be said for the ways of the administrator. Predictability in performance is the antithesis of the preferred working environment. A good example of the faculty viewpoint regarding the most desirable approach to institutional management was the dismay expressed by the Berkeley Commission on Governance over the practice followed by the University of California in relying on "administrative solutions" rather than on "a response of the committed group of faculty."[3] Within the university, therefore, we find both intrinsic and instrumental values, the faculty being the guardian of the former and the administrators tradesmen in the latter.

These sketches of the attitudes held by faculty and administrators are, of course, overdrawn. In the real world of any actual college or university, individual actors constitute a mix of the distinct qualities that have been attributed so starkly to each group. But these archetypes are useful when we attempt to examine some of the tensions that arise within a university. Starting with the sharply contrasting outlooks of the academician and the administrator, we can determine the origins of behavior and thereby explain the contending positions of those who would have their voices heard in the operation of our universities.

Faculty-Administration Tensions

The tensions that develop between faculty and administration are not always over matters of great importance. In fact, small incidents can spark bitter recrimination. Usually the occasion for dispute is when administrative style touches issues that contain symbolic implications. These situations occur when the academician is exposed to the bureaucratic process or when an administrator acts in such a way so as to emphasize within the educational program the relationship between the student and the college rather than between the student and the faculty. Invariably, the dispute is reduced to the issue of whether the institution takes precedence over the individual. "Governance" is the academician's shorthand for concern over such matters. The academic experience is replete with examples of this sore point.

Bureaucratic Process

The key to understanding the academician's perception of the bureaucratic process is to be found in his self-oriented behavior. His very style of performance creates a certain anxiety for him when his relationship with the university is defined in ways other than through ties to his department or links with his discipline. When he is confronted with the impersonal quality of the larger institution beyond his department, tensions develop. For the academician, "shared governance" is more than a shibboleth. It connotes the process by which an independent producer (himself) reaches an accommodation with the organizing principles of contemporary society. To begin with, academicians want to know who makes decisions and why. Without full disclosure, an otherwise justifiable decision can be viewed as an irresponsible act taken by a faceless bureaucrat, usually identified as a "clerk." The reaction is particularly sharp when the decision is taken beyond the largest administrative unit to which the individual academician regularly has access in seeking some explanation of the university's operations.

The curious aspect of such situations is the academician's response. He quickly feels a loss of dignity when confronted with bureaucratic practice. He is troubled by the anonymity of bureaucracy—bureaucrats having dealt with his request but not with him. Rather than by a personal letter expressing regret over the inability to accede to his request with some explanation for the decision, the news may be conveyed through little more than a form letter, or worse still, the word "disapproved" stamped across the face of his proposal. For the academician, with his self-oriented individualistic performance, the decision represents personal rejection.

More difficult situations develop when the basis of a decision on his application for promotion and tenure is not clear. Academicians can persistently press for the reasons for any failure to be promoted. Immediately the actor must be identified personally. The courts might uphold the administrator who responds that the negative decision was taken in his "best professional judgment." But for the academician this will not suffice. The only legitimate response is an objective recitation of any of his shortcomings, which he can then refute. Unlike those holding the bureaucratic perception, for the academician, the matter does not end with the decision.

The underlying problem is that most academicians do not understand how decisions are made in complex organizations. Because they interpret most actions taken in the name of the college from the viewpoint of their own independent and holistic style of working, they do not grasp the essence of the collective process. When a number of people working at different levels in a hierarchy are involved in making a decision, seldom is it possible to single out the voice that was critical to the result. Those who take part may never meet as a group. Compromises are made, and extraneous factors are brought into play along the way. The department evaluation committee, the dean, a vice-president, an all-college committee, and the president may share in the decision on an application for promotion, tenure, or even a sabbatical. As many as one hundred applications may be competing for attention. Each participant in the process has a point of view and makes a recommendation. The different levels of intensity that are expressed over one application or another and the relative prestige of each would-be decision maker within the college can influence the outcome. Perhaps the president must ultimately weigh all these factors. But when a resolution is achieved, who has made the decision? It is indeed difficult to say. Yet, because of the sense of personal rejection experienced by the academician from a denial of his application, it is almost as if he stands accused of not really being a practitioner of the academic art, and often he wants to identify and confront his accuser. The institutional dimension of decision making is lost on him, both in how it comes about and what the institution hopes to achieve in the decisions it makes. On the other side is the standpoint of an administrator, who sees that more is to be served in a decision than simply the interests of the candidate for promotion or tenure.

Bureaucracy in academia can always be counted upon to arouse feelings. During 1979, in a move to challenge the American Association of University Professors as the bargaining agent for the faculty of the state college system of Connecticut, the American Federation of Teachers raised this issue in one of its appeals: "We must start from a realistic appraisal of our situation—that of workers in a bureaucratized organization, far removed from the professionals we strive to be. A courageous and clear-cut stand on faculty needs is a precondition of professionalism. The present [situation] has given legal sanction to administrative paternalism rather than contributing to faculty self-determination."[4] Thus, the faculty perception of bureaucratic organization is revealed.

An important element of a bureaucratic stance is the argument that decisions of the past determine what is possible in the future. This assertion usually rests on considerations attached to the use of financial resources, and it is terribly frustrating for the academician. As an illustration, quotas for promotions or tenured faculty positions might have been set at a time of dire circumstance when there were declining enrollments and budget constraints. Or a limitation might have been placed on a percentage to be allowed in faculty salary increases. In the meantime, conditions have improved. But without consulting faculty, the president has devoted his new-found "surplus" to building a hockey rink or for some other purpose not directly related to the academic program and, therefore, to the faculty. The next time promotions or salary increases are discussed, the administrator voices the same limitations as before, but this time supported by different reasons. Institutional resources are still portrayed as being "tight" and fully committed. At this point, the president might claim that a foundation or a wealthy benefactor was prepared to build the hockey rink, but the college had to cover 25 percent of the cost. Surely the faculty did not want the college to lose such a substantial gift? Even though the academician might feel tricked, he will have a difficult time defying the logic of the administrator's position. Actually, he is only being exposed to (and in his sense manipulated by) an institutional and, therefore, bureaucratic perception. The issue of scarcity and the necessity for choices are always in the forefront of the administrator's argument. Both are prejudicial to the preferences of the academician. When he has not had a voice in any decision that impinges upon his sense of well-being, a dispute over governance usually cannot be avoided.

The struggle over governance between academicians and administrators has been apparent in the circumstances under which many faculties have established unions. With the opportunity offered by collective bargaining for expressing themselves to the public on the operation of the university, faculty at a variety of institutions have taken the occasion of strikes and picket lines to stress the importance of governance to their working environment. Early in 1979, in a challenge to President John Silber, representatives of the American Association of University Professors at Boston University led the faculty into a strike, largely because of the aggressive and directive style of the president. In taking this action, faculty spokesmen asserted that a settlement on salary could probably be reached, but first the administration must change its position and agree to discuss issues related to faculty participation in university governance.[5]

At the University of Bridgeport in October 1978, faculty also characterized their strike as an action they were forced to take because of differences with the administration over academic freedom, tenure, and governance. Because the two sides had agreed that union contracts must deal with "conditions of employment," the administration contended that bargaining should be limited to hours, wages, and working conditions. Governance was seen as an institutional matter. Although faculty participation in college decision making was not opposed by the administrators at Bridgeport, they contended that issues of collegiality did not belong in a union contract. The faculty representatives responded that the existing governance system gave final authority on every issue to the administration. Consequently, it was not acceptable.[6]

In effect, the academicians at Boston and Bridgeport were prepared to accept neither the legal fiction embodied in the corporate institution (and in which they had a voice as a constituent) nor the dual but separate identities which the administrators would have them assume as faculty and as a bargaining unit. In the idea of an omnipotent corporate university, faculty saw the vehicle of the administrators. In the concept of dual faculty identity, they saw the fragmentation of their influence. What the academicians at Boston and Bridgeport hoped to achieve was avoidance of the bureaucratic process. They wanted to identify the university with an independent faculty role in governance and to give legal status to that role by defining it in a collective bargaining agreement. Thereafter when administrators acted in some way which faculty believed was in violation of governance procedures, they would be subject to court action for contravening a contract.

Much the same battle occurred in developing the contract for the faculty in the state college system in Connecticut. Faculty insisted on giving legitimacy to the college senate by defining some of its prerogatives and functions in the collective bargaining agreement. Administrators again contended that the senate already had legitimacy from a number of years of practice and from the college by-laws approved by the broad of trustees. But the faculty would not be moved. Eventually, its view prevailed, largely because the negotiators for the state system did not fully grasp the significance of the union's purpose. In each of these cases, the administrators took an institutional perspective while the academicians hoped to avoid being enmeshed in the threatening institutional structure that allows so little latitude for decisions made by faculty.

Competition in Academic Programs

Another dimension of the tension prevalent in the academician's relationship with the university is in the structure of the academic program. Essentially, the issue is again whether the curriculum will be defined by the university—the vehicle of the administration—or the department—the institutional expression of the academician. This conflict is present in a number of forms. Normally the curriculum is considered the domain of the faculty. But because of the way academicians organize their work, part of the instruction they provide is beyond the purview of their immediate interests. This portion of the program may be general education or even an interdisciplinary honors program. In virtually all cases, it is presented to students as a feature of the college, not of the department or of the discipline with which the academician identifies. When administrators attempt to emphasize these aspects of the program, difficulty with faculty often ensues.

The issue constantly before the college is, of course, one of identity. Which will prevail, that of the independent practitioner or that of the institution? For the administrator, no conflict arises. In this, as in almost every other instance, he has no professional identity separate from his college or university. But for the academician, the matter is not so simple. Is he primarily a psychologist, biologist, economist—or is he first a "college teacher"? Many academicians prefer the former identity and like to look upon their teaching as almost the outgrowth of this professional status. Even then, some see their instructional role not as teaching so much as imparting particular knowledge to neophytes. They view the administrator who presses for extradisciplinary commitments as someone who contributes to their loss of identity and prestige.

A variation of the struggle over academic program and identity is also to be seen at the few colleges that have adopted competency-based degrees. Although this number is not great, the example it provides is instructive for all of higher education because this type of curriculum creates vivid tensions between academician and administrator. Under these programs, faculty still instruct and certify student achievement with grades, but the development of student competence is not necessarily associated with the classroom—the academician's normal mode of expression as an instructor. Emphasis is on the student's rather than the instructor's role. The organizing principle is that of the college, as an institution, providing the environment in which students' learning takes place. The student has the initiative to draw on its resources as he sees fit. Departments, and at times even the discipline, become secondary. Interdisciplinary programs abound as students' imagination is given free reign. In such cases, the instructor can be reduced to merely a learning resource.

When a competence-based curriculum was adopted in the late 1970s at Alverno College, a small Catholic women's institution in Milwaukee, some faculty quickly concluded that their autonomy was being threatened. Administrators responded that malcontents within the faculty refused to commit themselves to the institutional task of overhauling the college's educational program. Faculty were frightened, the dean claimed, because student development would be measured by someone other than the academician providing the instruction. Students, in fact, could measure their own progress in ways other than through the grades they received. In this process, the work of the individual faculty member could be assessed independently of what he himself might say about his performance. The threat which the dean implied was that any faculty ineffectiveness that might exist could no longer be concealed. An institutional assessment of degree candidates would replace the usual practice of determining student achievement by an array of grades in forty or more courses—the fragmented evaluation provided by individual instructors.

In turn, faculty members at Alverno raised the issue that always comes to the surface when academicians are threatened by the institution—governance. Their claim was that academic freedom was being violated, dissent suppressed, and as teachers they were denied an adequate role in shaping academic policy. Generally, they felt that they had no power in decision making. One instructor even claimed that anti-intellectualism was rampant, that administrators despised publishing and research, and that being at Alverno was like living in a concentration camp.[7] There can be little doubt from these figures of speech that the institutional aspects of a college or university loom large for faculty under these conditions. At Colgate University a similar program was instituted in the early 1970s, but it fell into disuse from faculty neglect for many of the same reasons as were voiced by the academicians at Alverno. The difference at Colgate was that the administrators, whether in unusual wisdom or because of a recognized lack of authority to perform the task, did not attempt to compel the faculty to support the program.

Many of the same fears were expressed when an effort was made to institute an honors program at Central Connecticut State College. In this case, the proposal included (1) an intensive team-taught interdisciplinary seminar of one or two years duration on the experience, culture, and values of Western civilization; (2) the development of student competency in mathematics or a foreign language; (3) monthly discussions for students with select faculty; and (4) whatever tutorials departments wished to organize for honors program students who happened to be their majors. The principal objection of those who opposed the proposal was to the highly irregular procedure of its having originated in the dean's office. In fact, it was the idea of the associate dean. In the history of the college (and the college was 132 years old), no one could cite a case in which a dean had ever submitted a proposal to the curriculum committee.

Only slightly beneath the surface of debate was the view that the main features of the proposal unnecessarily deemphasized the role of departments. In a memorandum circulated by the History Department, the college community was told that honors programs at other colleges were decentralized, being supervised by individual departments. The salient aspect of the historians' argument hinged on the administration of the program—who would select the faculty to teach the interdisciplinary seminar, determine student acceptance into the program, set the required levels of achievement necessary for students to remain in it, and ascertain competence that would be necessary for successful completion? The real issue was one of governance. Obviously, for many academicians, the program was too institutional in its structure. Conceivably, it could operate to the detriment of departments. The dean was seen as being too active in an area normally reserved for faculty initiative.

Other difficulties can also develop that pit the individual academician against the institution over educational matters. Any move by an administrator, for example, to change grades unilaterally on the basis of a student's plea is perceived as institutional interference in the classroom. An administrator's being assigned the task of supervising (and therefore evaluating) student performance in an experiential program of field work, cooperative education, or internship may also be challenged. In one instance departments refused to use a director of cooperative education for the placement of their interns even though he had excellent contacts in the community and could have greatly facilitated their work. Explanations of this attitude were difficult to obtain, but essentially the faculty's position rested on a suspicion that this assistance would allow institutional intercession into academic matters. In such cases, the administrator is often seen by faculty as standing behind institutional intercession to serve a public perception that is the antithesis of academic thinking.

Faculty Instruments of Power

Thus far in this explanation, only the defensive aspects of faculty posture toward the institution with which the academician is affiliated have been considered. What of faculty initiatives? In its relationship with the college, the faculty is not without influence. Its power is derived from intellectual competence and scholarly commitment. As seen by the general public, colleges and universities are a reserve of high-level manpower suitable for a variety of purposes. When special talent is required, the university is one of the first places industry and government seek it. Over the past generation, college professors have become a fixture in just about every administration in Washington, serving as advisers, holding cabinet posts, and staffing the large number of regulatory agencies that have become a part of our complex society.

The quality that allows academicians to acquire high positions is the influence they achieve from being seen as those who would formulate answers to the many questions that trouble our society. Essentially, they occupy this place because they write books on social, cultural, and scientific matters whereas most other people do not. It may be that through some sort of collective intuition society does, after all, grasp the academic truth—that the essence of the proper academic life is creativity and that the profession is organized to allow the participant the time for inventive pursuits. Over the years, individual academicians have developed an association with society that does not depend upon the administrators of their universities. The academician as well as the university becomes known. Having acquired reputation, the academician can claim authority within his institution because of the prestige he brings to it. To the extent that a university depends upon the reputation of its faculty, the academician will have a voice in its business.

When authority within the university is measured by academic prestige, it is the administrator who experiences restrictions in his claims to jurisdiction over its affairs. The most significant qualification on an administrator's efforts to vie with faculty for influence is that his ties to academic subject matter are at best tangential. Leadership cannot be derived from spontaneous faculty consent based on some contribution that the administrator makes to the group product. Most administrators cannot assume that their claims to authority will be affirmed through faculty appreciation of the administrator's role in the organization. Only in the professionalism of the myriad of disciplines that constitute a university does the academician acknowledge authority. The administrator has few ways to qualify for this legitimacy. It would be different if he continued intellectual work in an academic discipline while tending to the affairs of the college. But alas, the distance from the administration building to the science laboratory is indeed greater than might be expected.

But an unexpected source of difficulty occurs for the academician. Prestige within academia carries far beyond the individual or specific group generating it. To some degree, the entire profession benefits. Mancur Olson provides a useful analogy in likening a collective benefit to a public good.[8] The benefit—in this case, society's respect for academia and its willingness to support academic activities—is in some ways indivisible. The well-known academician who is sought after by government and foundations is the originator of the product, but he cannot exclude other academicians from reaping some of the advantage he creates. At this level of consideration, the faculty can assume a corporate as opposed to a departmental identity. Among academicians, return in the form of prestige is not always proportionate to output. There is a systematic tendency for exploitation of the great by the small. The group will contend that the influence afforded some faculty members must be generalized to the entire collegium. Thus, the inconsequential academician is able to benefit from the milieu afforded by the company of colleagues who are recognized scholars.

Because of this circumstance, an academician often has difficulty making accurate assessments of his position at the university with which he is affiliated. And quite frankly, administrators take faculty pretensions less seriously. Tucked away at a small college in the perfect and blissful isolation of the Pine Barrens or the Chenango Valley, an academician may become unrealistic about his particular situation. He sometimes concludes that despite his insignificance nationally, at home he should have more influence and prestige than he actually enjoys. If he loses battles with administrators, he questions the legitimacy of the outcome, develops an adversary complex, and sees manipulation and underhanded practices on the part of those who do not share his point of view on a particular issue.

The peculiarity of the academician's perspective is that he tends to interpret his specific set of circumstances in loosely construed views regarding the entire academic profession. On any occasion, he may focus on problems which academia's leading spokesmen perceive as applying to the sector as a whole or to American's prestigious universities. All the while he ignores the actual issues before his own college. He can become exercised over salaries even though his pay scale is well above that at competing institutions. When faculty job security is an issue on the national scene, he can publicly abhor the failure of his college to retain some faculty member, while privately agreeing that the individual in question is of such low professional caliber that it was a mistake to have hired him in the first place. He can fret over his loss of power to administrators and students because of reports that this phenomenon is occurring elsewhere even though the faculty at his college has as much authority as ever in determining educational policy.

This tendency need not be considered a mystery. An academician's institutional relationships and perceptions are derived from his capacity as a professional for transcending his immediate environment. As already noted, working techniques permit an individual to identify more closely with members of his discipline wherever they may be than with those with whom he has spatial continuity at his university of employment. This larger circle becomes his point of reference and he naturally sees most situations in its terms.

When specific issues are fashioned from general but inapplicable conditions, proposed solutions or demands are not formulated by the faculty with a view to an outcome that might reasonably be expected from discussion, negotiation, or bargaining. Political action becomes symbolic. At times, an outside observer might suspect that the faculty derives more satisfaction from proving some abstract point about the level of academic salaries than from actually getting a pay raise. Wherever this disposition exists, it has serious implications for the administrator who sees the world in terms of institutional purpose. Permitting the academician to define the issue can lead to a fairyland of imagined concerns.

The academician's reliance on prestige for influence within his university provides a good context for exploring his singular approach to politics in an institutional setting. In not recognizing the tenuous nature of the link between prestige and influence, many academicians fail to understand the nature of politics. The newcomer to academic circles who has experience in the bureaucratic reaches of government or corporate life can be properly confounded by the academicians' inclination to see the distribution of power as stacked against them, being held by an assortment of administrators who supposedly can control the turn of events with little more than a nod of the head or the pointing of an index finger. The academician's belief is that because the faculty—or he himself—has prestige, the university should accommodate his wishes. The uncertainties of this approach to power are not difficult to see. Its configuration, which the academician devises because of his compulsion for autonomy, is the source of his trepidation over institutions, particularly the one with which he is associated. His claim to authority lacks a mechanism for translating faculty prestige into institutional power. The exercise of the academician's power depends on the acquiescence, interpretations, and actions of administrators. To the academician, the university constantly appears to be in the hands of others.

Throughout this assessment of the relative influences of the academician and the administrator within the university, one factor has always been present in the background—the ties that each group maintains with society beyond the confines of the institution the two have in common. These links largely determine the sway that each will hold over the affairs of the university. In most cases, administrators are perceived as having the advantage in any contest for control of the institution, and it is no wonder. The administrator interprets his role as applying to the institution as a whole. He negotiates with the forces of society for the purpose of acquiring the resources necessary to carry out the academic functions performed within the university. In so doing, he has been able to capture the identity of the university insofar as the public is concerned.

One of the contradictions in which the academician finds himself is voiced in a standard complaint against administrators. Rather than seeing themselves as interpreters of education to the public, the academician will assert, administrators are more intent on interpreting the concerns of business and industry to the faculty. The essence of this charge is that administrators should perform the service of selling to the public the educational product as devised according to academic concepts. Most academicians maintain that administrators should avoid an all-too-common practice of attempting to reshape the educational program in some way that suits the ever-changing perception of the public. The academicians' dilemma, of course, is to be found in the association the administrator establishes with the public while performing the service function ordained for him by the faculty. From this association the administrator may develop a proclivity for the public's view of education.

If the administrator in recent years has had the upper hand because of his association with the public, this has not always been the case. A force that for some years ran counter to centralization and the enhancement of administrative authority was the financial support that government and foundations gave directly to individual academicians through research grants, particularly to the specialized institutes located at the great universities. In many instances, this flow of resources was virtually beyond the reach of the administrator. With federal and foundation grants, professors—in their capacity as institute directors or grant administrators—controlled much of the academic income, leave time, and administrative support funds that were available within a university. Insofar as a faculty member had direct access to the resources for financing travel, hiring professionals, and acquiring equipment, the individual academician could even determine the new programs that would be initiated at his university.

A university administrator in such instances was left to confirm the directions in which the affluent professoriate chose to take the institution. In effect, the prestige of the outstanding faculty members permitted the academician to circumvent some of the restrictions associated with relying on the administrator for the institutional support that otherwise is necessary for scholarly activity. It was indeed difficult for a president or academic vice-president to tell faculty that they must refuse a grant because it goes beyond the mission of the university or generates maintenance and other overhead costs that exceed the institution's long-range capacity to cover.

This situation demonstrates the validity of the assertion that the public domain can greatly affect intramural decisions and power relationships through its ability to determine who within the university will control financial resources. From the time of the success of the Soviet Union in missilery and atomic weaponry until the late 1960s, the public's inclination in funding higher education favored the professor over the administrator. Academia was faculty-oriented. Sometimes it almost seemed as if the benefactors were not concerned with the results their research grants might produce. It was enough for corporations, foundations, and government to provide the financing and permit the academician to determine how effective his use of the money might be.

By the mid-1970s, the public's mood had changed appreciably. General support for higher education continued. In what the professoriate perceived as relatively lean times, the total revenue of all types of colleges and universities increased by 11.2 percent in 1976, 9.7 percent in 1977, 8.3 percent in 1978, 9.6 percent in 1979, and 11.9 percent in 1980. For 1981 the increase was estimated at 14 percent.[9] The difference was that government and foundation assistance now had more of a student bias. Many government agencies began to question the payoff from the research funds they funneled into academe. Instead of discrete faculty projects for small atomic reactors, electronic language laboratories, and the like, direct government grants began to be made to universities to meet expenses associated with teaching programs as opposed to research potential. Foundations provided institutional grants in relation to innovative undergraduate curriculum and the education of minorities. A large portion of public funds went into state and community colleges that emphasized teaching over research.

Another sign of the public's disposition was the proposed income tax rebate for college tuition that was debated vociferously but not adopted by Congress in 1978. To the extent that it benefited academia at all, the advantage would have been to the institution, which then might have had more leeway in raising tuition. Higher faculty salaries could result, but once again the controlling factor would be the institution and its administration rather than faculty with its professional identity. The trend was away from resources being controlled by the individual research-directed academician and toward the public's financing of student-slanted activities under the supervision of administrators. Research activities were still being financed, but when compared with faculty expectations and with the size of the engine that academicians had built over the years, funding seemed scant. The arbiters of such funds no longer had an interest in supporting the academician's search for whatever his mind was capable of grasping. The perfect, ever-expanding intellectual environment which the academician found so conducive to the Cartesian spirit of inquiry was no longer the object of so much largesse.

The question that arises from this situation is: In view of his prestige with the public, why was the academician unable to capture at least a portion of the image of the university? The principal difficulty was that within its perception of formal authority, the public could not identify most of the claims of the individual academician. The academician's service to the college through governance is an internal activity which the public seldom sees. Neither is the academician's role as a teacher clearly discernible outside the college. Within the academy itself, one faculty member or another may have the reputation of being a great teacher, but the general public subsumes teaching under the impersonal heading of instruction, a mission society identifies with the college rather than with the individual who provides this service.

Thus, one of the few roles in which academicians are recognized by the public is in research, and then only when they become noted as authors or authorities. But in providing professional service outside the college, the academician functions in a way that is truly extraneous to the college. He is usually so intent upon pursuing his individual interests that he seldom goes out of his way to identify this service with his place of employment. Consequently, he is not in a position to extract from the university a quid pro quo for professional reputation that reflects positively on that institution. When outside resources begin to shift away from faculty controlled activities, the professoriate, as independent practitioners, does not maintain a hold on the authority which the resource flow has up to this point allowed it. Academicians do not give permanence to this aspect of their performance. They do not "institutionalize" it, so to speak. To do so would constitute a distraction from their Cartesian mission. Whenever external resources shrink, therefore, faculty are compelled to return to reliance on their respective universities for support. Their scholarly activities must then be financed by endowment, tuition, state budgets, or federal and foundation monies that are channeled through the university rather than directly to the academician.

Quasi-Administration

The independent-minded academician does have a response to the bureaucratic effectiveness of the administrator. He perceives the operation of the collective embodied in the university as quasi-administration that can be performed by faculty itself. This is a device by which decision-making authority is appropriated by those who otherwise consider themselves teachers and researchers. Quasi-administration is defined by the maximum administrative role faculty as a group can play if they are all to be involved and if each is also to teach and retain the freedom to pursue research and professional activity. By definition, quasi-administration is a part-time pursuit. To go beyond this point, that is, to have some faculty accept a specialized administrative role, is to alienate these individuals from the collegium—to turn them into administrators, from whence the struggle between the academician and his institution will begin anew. Inherent to quasi-administration is an effort to avoid charging anyone with performing administrative duties on a full-time basis.

When brought face to face with authority and confronted by the necessity to work within a large institution, the academician responds with a defensive mechanism that is fully recognized in social theory. Max Weber alluded to it as antiauthoritarian forms of organization by which participants attempt to reduce the imperative associated with execution (or administration) by (1) ending specialization of executive functions; (2) treating an office as an avocation, not a full-time occupation; (3) allowing incumbents only a short time in office; and (4) giving all members of the collective a term of office through rotation, or perhaps even selection by lot.[10]

These concepts are well known in academia as techniques for limiting an administrator's power. They are often applied to a department chairman and sometimes even to deans. One faculty committee charged with restructuring the deanship of a small elite Eastern university followed Weber's prescription almost perfectly in recommending that the dean should be from the faculty, hold office for only five years, have his appointment approved by a majority of his peers, and continue to teach while performing his administrative duties. A variety of reasons associated with the well-being of the college was given for each stipulation. Actually, it was a time when tensions were high over faculty assertions that the president was exercising undue power on matters affecting educational policy. In responding to the situation, the faculty committee demonstrated almost perfect proclivity for Weber's antiauthoritarian form of organization. In defining the charge to the dean, the faculty members were not thinking of administrative responsibilities. They were attempting to make the position the head of their own quasi-administration.

In his consideration of collegia, Weber treated quasi-administration in his observation that government by amateurs means extensive as opposed to intensive administration. It favors thoroughness in weighing administrative decisions, but involves obstacles to precise, clear, and rapid action.[11] Current university practice, in instances where faculty have influence over administrative decisions, will attest to the accuracy of Weber's analysis. Deliberations are lengthy, they embody a relatively large number of individuals, and the outcome is seldom clear. Weber saw the ultimate result of quasi-administration being the division of responsibility in the collegium to a point where accountability disappears almost entirely. This condition is also characteristic of academic organization. Here again, faculty behavior can be explained as a function of small group activity. As group relationships become more diffuse and affective, it is less likely that leadership will be charged with taking on specific well-defined tasks. Academicians resist any effort by the administrator to achieve a sufficient concentration of authority to perform what he considers to be normal organizational functions.

Literature on American universities abounds with examples of the professoriate's insistence on quasi-administrative functions being afforded the faculty. Dressel's survey confirmed that departments prefer to handle as they see fit all business linked to their activities—and with a minimum of accountability to the larger institution.[12] The 1967 Report of the University of California Commission on Governance provided innumerable examples of this attitude. Probably the clearest expression was the assertion that a department or institute should be permitted to determine both admission and course requirements for students enrolled in its program, to hire its own nonacademic staff, and to make its own resource allocations.[13] Barzun noted the occurrence of quasi-administration in the practice of allowing faculty committees to make decisions on appointment, tenure, and promotion.[14]

In quasi-administration, the full aspects of administration—planning, budgeting, staffing, and program implementation—are seldom considered. Through a plethora of committees, individual faculty members attempt to make decisions on the basis of limited information and without full consideration of the implications that devolve upon those having executive burdens. Usually there is a unidimensional quality about quasi-administration as attention is devoted to the concerns of only one department, or perhaps of the corporate faculty in isolation from students, administrators, or the public.

Academicians contend that at the level of the university as a whole, their decisions should be the principal, if not the exclusive, determinant in the shaping of educational policy. Disputes can easily arise over whether an issue has policy implications and consequently over whether administrators standing outside the collegial structure can rightfully proceed with self-assigned tasks before consulting the various committees of the university that claim policy-making authority. The problem is particularly troublesome because no matter what the situation, faculty are ever alert to the sacrifice of values to expediency. They believe that any time values are at stake, the issue is one of policy. As a consequence, nothing is routine. Policy considerations become involved in even the most ordinary administrative decisions.

Herbert Simon noted that whenever executive functions are pursued in terms of broad human values, accountability virtually disappears, a consequence that Weber saw ensuing from quasi-administration.[15] Thus the circle is squared. The academician's self-oriented behavior, his penchant for value-laden determinations, and the compulsion to follow the practices of antiauthoritarian organization each serves to reinforce the other and to produce the curiosities of academia's quasi-administration. The only trouble with this mode of operation is that it is more appropriate for a medieval corporate guildlike enterprise than for an institution that must process the claims of thousands of students. In fact, society's bureaucratic norms of the last years of the twentieth century have become far removed from the entrepreneurial and Cartesian purposes of the academician.

The way faculty talk about their participation in quasi-administration may seem unusual to the outsider. While devoting immeasurable time to college committee work, the academician will complain about the waste it involves and express a desire to reduce his commitment. One view of faculty behavior, which tends to discount complaints about the inordinate amount of time consumed in quasi-administration, was developed by Alvin Gouldner twenty-five years ago. Gouldner believed academicians fall into two categories—"locals" who are teachers with low commitment to their disciplines insofar as they do not have much published research and "cosmopolitans" who are recognized as successful conveyors of knowledge through their disciplines. The former have no prestige outside the college at which they are employed, whereas the latter have professional associations throughout society and are sought after for their professional expertise. This is roughly the same division that was borrowed from Mancur Olson, Jr., to explain how the great can be exploited by the small in the distribution of goods and benefits within a collective. Gouldner characterizes "locals" as those who devote a large portion of their time to governance bodies and quasi-administration while the "cosmopolitans" avoid faculty meetings and institutional assignments in order to spend their time on research, writing, and disciplinary as opposed to institutional ties.[16]

Gouldner's findings suggest that the cosmopolitans enjoy individual bargaining power with the administration because of their prestige. As a result, they have little reason to seek collective power through quasi-administration. According to this line of reasoning, there is an implied community of interests between the two. The cosmopolitans find a strong administration acceptable because it assures the orderly arrangements under which their work flourishes. From the standpoint of the administrator, the cosmopolitans further the mission of the college. The recognition they achieve from the public or in professional circles adds luster to the college's image. They are the producers; they deserve whatever rewards are available. Quite simply, the administrator is willing to provide what the cosmopolitans want because their activities can be interpreted within the institutional setting of the administration, even though the cosmopolitan's motives are totally individual.

The concept of the university expressed through quasi-administration is identified by the administrator with the participating locals—people of lesser prestige. Quasi-administration becomes secondary in the minds of administrators insofar as it is not associated with the best faculty. Locals are perceived as meddlers because of their insistence on dabbling in what the administrator considers his work. There is no neat and efficient division of labor (an administrative perception) between administrator and local as there is with cosmopolitans. Herein may lie a broad if somewhat theoretical explanation for the rise of faculty unionism. Administrators resist the quasi-administration of locals, who respond with attempts to maximize their institutional power by organizing themselves more along the bureaucratic lines of the administrator.

Rationalizing Administrative Structure

Considering the diverse perceptions—even the different worlds—of the academician and the administrator, can the individual mission of the one ever become compatible with the institutional responsibilities of the other? Whether it is possible or not, this objective is the only plausible principle by which the academic administrator can organize his work. The task has two parts. First is the necessity to structure the administration of the college in a way that facilitates an improved working atmosphere between the two. Second, the administrator must adopt a style that permits him to serve the institutional objectives of the university while showing due sensitivity for the perceptions of the academician.

An organizational trend that has been present in academia since the mid-1970s seems to indicate that movement is under way to achieve the first of these purposes. Few academicians have not observed the inordinate increase in the number of administrators, even while the college-age population (and therefore the number of potential students) is about to decline. Although the creation of new administrative posts is usually criticized by faculty as a step toward the bureaucratization of the academy, there has been a certain logic behind the development. Much of the new bureaucratic structure is a response to the necessity to meet the administrative requirements placed on a university's senior officers—the president and vice-presidents—by the pressure for public accountability as outside management has become more pervasive. The new types of positions that have appeared include material coordinators, patent coordinators, directors of external grants, directors of risk management, compliance officers, deans of institutional advancement, and deans of personnel. The establishing of this final position was a move prompted partially by faculty unionization and the concomitant necessity to manage collective bargaining contracts.

If the academician sees bureaucratization going too far in the university, it is within academic affairs, where directors of individualized instruction, directors of freshmen programs, directors of short courses/seminars, and deans of instruction are now employed.[17] The rationale for these positions is to assure that certain secondary features of the curriculum receive more attention than when they are left solely to the deans of schools such as arts and sciences, business, and education. These new positions are viewed with alarm by many academicians because they are extraneous to the departmental collegia. They represent the institutional aspect of the instructional program as opposed to traditional courses, which are left to the initiative of faculty working within disciplines. As a result, they are identified with undue institutional or administrative interference into the prerogatives of the faculty.

Actually, the new positions have another purpose: they perform coordinating roles; they have responsibility for functions rather than for staffs or subdivisions of the university; and they usually serve the vice-president for academic affairs. Many vice-presidents rely on such a staff because it permits them to keep their hand on the internal operations of the college while devoting a large portion of their time to the new and additional concerns of dealing with outsider management. These staff positions are a result, therefore, of the administrative superstructure that has been imposed on higher education by external forces in recent years. A vice-president must now have two sets of eyes. The new staff officers are meant to serve as a check on the initiative of academic deans, whose line of responsibility within the organization gives them discretionary authority that can be exercised with excessive exuberance now that the vice-president must focus his attention more on the external concerns of the college. With faculties of business, arts and sciences, and education all pursuing independent paths, the program of the college as a whole can lose its coherence without some extension of the vice-president's authority.

But there is another way of looking at this phenomenon. In academic affairs the administrator literally sits between two cultures. One is that of our dependent entrepreneur—the academician guided by his Cartesian principles. The other is our pluralistic society with its concepts of efficiency, group achievement, and competition. In response to the situation, academic administrators have begun operating more as teams with greater specialization on the part of team members. Under the new division of labor among academic administrators, academic deans manage human resources—the faculty— while vice-presidents manage material resources as represented by budgets, institutional planning, and building programs. The new positions merely extend the vice-president's authority over the entire institution.

Academic deans now occupy the half step between the department and the senior administration. In a classic sense, they are middle management. Department chairmen are also drawn into this middle position. Together deans and chairmen constitute the level of administration that is critical to the implementation of educational programs and to the enhancement of the academician's professional and instructional activities. Ideas on possible innovations—new research, new courses—are vetted. The resources that are needed to undertake these innovations are identified. At this level in the administration, an effort is made to channel whatever energy and initiative the faculty embodies into activities that will work to the benefit of both the university and the academician.

Thus the decisions made by a dean have more immediate impact on the day-to-day activities of the individual academician than do those of the vice-president. The latter's influence is in setting the administrative tone of the university. The determinations of the former are at the margin, choices that point much more directly at one department or even at one individual faculty member than another—more equipment for the art or music department and less for the natural sciences; a new interpretation of laboratory fees that allows the geography department to dip into this source of financing to develop a regional planning program; a reallocation of monies from the supply account to honoraria for outside speakers or possibly for sponsoring a regional conference in psychology; moving faculty positions from history to social work as the older academicians retire in the former department and student demand develops in the latter; responding to the decline in student interest in foreign language by permitting the language laboratory to fall into disuse as the cassettes wear out and the tape recorders get beyond repair; allocating a faculty position to a remedial writing center; encouraging physics to begin a program in solar energy; signaling that henceforth funds available for promotion will be used only to reward professionally active faculty; deciding how limited travel funds will be apportioned; denying one but approving another request for released time; setting priorities for sabbatical leave.

These are the sorts of decisions over which deans usually have discretion. They also relate directly to the work of the academician. In any instance, a vice-president can reverse a dean's decision, but seldom does it come to that. The decisions taken by deans are highly visible, and their significance can be grasped by the academician from his limited institutional perspective. They carry none of the mysteries for faculty of the overall university budget where sinking funds, "set-asides" for increases in fuel oil prices, overtime funds for snow removal, cash reserves, short-term commercial paper transactions, and the like can confound the intelligence of the ordinary mortal who would otherwise devote his attention to Greek philosophy, nineteenth-century English literature, or limnology.

Administrative Style

To a large extent, it is the manner in which a decision is carried out rather than the content of the decision itself that determines how an academician might respond to it. Style is important. And in any consideration of academic style, it is appropriate to focus attention on academic deans. The same rules may apply to other administrators. But with deans, there is the element of constant human contact between administration and faculty. The dean is the first level of administration to be encountered by the academician, and it is at this point that the impression is created of administration being an annoyance or a source of support. In this discussion, an attempt will be made to give an operational flavor to some of the concepts that were developed earlier.

In dealing with the faculty, a dean often starts with a handicap. One strong faculty perception is that no one beyond the confines of the department should make decisions having adverse ramifications for

an individual academician ad hominum. Thus, approval or disap-
proval of an individual's application for promotion, sabbatical, or travel
funds should carry the strong imprint of the department as expressed
by colleagues within the discipline. Many academicians will never
quite accept the idea that an administrator can rightfully reverse such a
decision of their peers. In their view, decisions taken by those beyond
the discipline should be limited to such matters as the level of resources to be allocated to the department as a group, and then only if
rewards and denials are apportioned from one department to another
according to the academician's concept of balance. Because a dean
operates in both areas, in the realm of a direct and personal relationship with the individual academician as well as on the indirect and
disciplinary concerns of the department, he assumes his duties knowing that certain tensions are part of his relationship with faculty.

Seldom can the academician's view of administrative propriety be
accommodated within the institutional goals and administrative practices of a university. Whatever faculty might think, there must be an
overview of the organization that cannot be derived simply from the
conglomeration of departmental preferences. Moreover, a dean cannot
be a man of all seasons. At any particular time, he cannot relate to all
disciplines identically. In performing his functions, however, he must
attempt to deal with faculty in ways that help give this impression.

Faculty often characterize a popular dean as a "faculty man," which
simply means that he acts within the limits of the proposition that the
faculty is the university. This perception places the academic administrator in a much more confined position than those who hold middle
management positions outside academia. Business and government
executives—even at the middle levels—are different insofar as they
commit themselves to responsibility for what their organizations
might become. The status quo has little meaning for them. They
assume a sense of detachment so they can view the institution's future
distinct from its present and past. They place a high premium on being
dispassionate in their decisions. In so doing, they suppose that their
judgment will be sharpened. And when they call for action in any part
of the organization, they expect to have action first and questions
afterward. Such an outlook is the antithesis of faculty thinking. The
academician holds that only through commitment to the intrinsic
values of which the faculty is protector can proper direction be given to
the university. From this point of view comes the academician's perception of the administrator occupying a service function. "Good"

deans serve faculty values. They are guided by the Cartesian principles, which allow all who work within their purview to seek whatever knowledge their minds are capable of grasping.

When undue tension occurs between faculty and an administrator, whether it be with a dean, vice-president, or president, the problem may be that the academician sees that individual following a course in his administrative behavior which has been identified in a preceding paragraph with business executives. The one case in which academic administration became a public issue of near national scope occurred at Boston University, where the president, John Silber, was involved in what at times appeared to be a raucous alley brawl with much of the faculty. Silber ably defended his position on the national feature news show "60 Minutes" in January 1980. He talked the public's language, whereas the faculty's message was so alien to the public's ear that it was barely comprehensible.

In a subsequent interview, Silber appeared to be sensitive to the charge that he operated Boston University as if it were a business. In response to the accusation, he contended that a university is, in fact, a corporation. "A budget has to be balanced," he said, "simply because an institution is a responsible organization...BU [Boston University] is run like a corporation; it has to be. But it is a very special kind of corporation that sells special services—educational services and re-search services." At the same time, Silber denied that he saw the university as a business that had to be operated for purposes of profit. In identifying his greatest contribution to the university, he added, "I think it has been making the right diagnosis, knowing what's wrong with the place, and knowing what had to be done to correct it." Generally, Silber's view was one of wrenching the university on to a new (and sustained) course—doing whatever was necessary to assure its academic integrity and to respond to the segment of the public that desired quality education. Silber gave the university primacy over the faculty, which in his scheme of things occupied a subsidiary role. It was clear that he saw absolutely no merit in collective bargaining units as a vehicle for giving faculty a voice in the operation of the university. In fact, he conveyed the impression of holding the entire idea and those faculty who supported it in utter contempt. For faculty, Boston University under Silber was indeed being managed as if it were a business.[18]

If Silber had a difficulty, it was his virtual defiance of the academic perception. The controlling feature of the administrator-faculty rela-tionship may be likened to an implied contract capsulized within the concept of academic freedom. At least, this is the customary position taken by the academician when he perceives an administrator exceeding the bounds established by the Cartesian principles. As it relates to a university's operation, the contract's most prominent feature is the administrator's presuming to show deference toward and provide a guardianship for the academician's time. It is perhaps in that measure of worth that an unintended source of conflict can arise. Whereas the administrator sees the world in terms of resource flows, the academician calculates in units of time.

The administrator who appreciates this difference and operates under its premise has taken a big step toward establishing the atmosphere in which the values of society and those of the academy can live side by side. Although the two standards can never be totally reconciled, a scale of conversion does appear to exist. Faculty responsibilities can be divided into two parts—the social mission of the university present in lower-level instruction combined with university service, and the autonomous mission of the academician found in research, in teaching esoteric seminars, or in the individual pursuit of ideas. In the operation of a university, the social mission of the faculty (and the claims it makes on the academician's time) can be balanced against the level of financial support that administrators can generate from the public for the autonomous mission of the academician. Thus is the bargain struck. The administrator is largely responsible for striking it and for operating within its conditions.

At this point, we encounter the matter of administrative style. In administration, success does not necessarily depend upon all those within an institution agreeing with a decision taken by an administrator. Just as often, it is contingent upon the constituencies concluding that the actor knows what he is doing. Within a highly individualized, vocal, and cerebral institution such as a university, the successful administrator usually keeps the channels of communications with faculty relatively busy, conveying to the academician the essence of his actions and decisions, not so much through regulations, memorandums, and formal announcements as in personal comments to individuals with whom he has regular contact. The holding of a well-formed viewpoint on the part of the administrator about the academic endeavor can help shape the content of these messages. Success for an administrator in working with academicians on university matters can be promoted by the implicit observation of the Cartesian principles. Even actions that do not relate directly to the six rules that were posited in Chapter 2 can usually be interpreted according to them. The opportunity to set the context of decisions cannot be ignored. For an administrator to preempt the interpretation of his actions is often to assure faculty acceptance of them.

The steps involved in this maneuver are first to determine what must be done, then to develop an explanation for it that is consistent with the Cartesian perception, and finally to assure wide dissemination of the message. The process is clearly political. If questions arise, sometimes nothing more is necessary than for the administrator to acknowledge the validity of the principle of the academic perception that is at issue. Just this one symbolic act may be enough to reduce tensions. The real art is in getting the academician to accept the administrator's definition of the situation.

Above all else, signals must be clear. The obfuscation that is sometimes useful within a bureaucracy will serve an administrator poorly in academia. Perhaps nothing is more galling to the academician than to be taken by surprise by some move on the part of the administration which indicates that the collegium has been bypassed. The concept "faculty as university" has not been honored. In a university, an administrator must convey the impression of being aware that he is working with individuals and not with units in a hierarchy. From the faculty standpoint, anyone who is influenced by a decision—particularly the dependent enterpreneur—deserves that much consideration. When this acknowledgment is not forthcoming, the administrator will bear the bruises of the challenge that he has been "capricious and arbitrary," a phrase without which contemporary academic dialogue would probably not endure.

In earlier pages, the contention was made that the academician relates poorly to the institution by which he is employed. This condition is not surprising for someone who is engaged in independent and holistic activity and whose most important point of reference is his discipline rather than his institution of employment. A large part of what an administrator does when he works with faculty is to interpret the institution for them. He tries to make the impersonal monster which the academician sees in any organization less threatening. Thereafter, the administrator can often count on the entrepreneurial spirit of individual faculty members to achieve the mission of the university. Thus academic administration can be nondirective. It is not necessary to tell academicians constantly what to do. If clear signals are given by the university's senior administrators, a sufficient number of faculty will be ready to work for the prescribed purpose to assure a task's completion. All they require is to be informed of the direction the university is going and permitted to accept work freely on terms they consider legitimate. The purpose of the administrator is to structure situations in such a way to allow for the furthering of the university's program under these conditions. Admittedly, it involves an element of manipulation insofar as the administrator must also avoid the academician's penchant for disassembling the institution.

If some change in the characteristics of the university is deemed necessary, the administration will usually find advantage in observing the formalities of process which acknowledge faculty preeminence in matters of educational policy. When institutional interests must take precedence, they are advanced in terms of faculty sufferance. Time is always allowed for new ideas to be explored and for the faculty to indicate its accord. As a result, reform proceeds at a snail's pace. It is seldom advisable for the administrator to take the initiative in sponsoring new approaches. Rather, he must appear to perform a coordinating or facilitating function for those faculty who wish him to do so. For the faculty, he obviously sees the university as they do. In deliberations with faculty, an administrator usually does well to suppress his concern for larger institutional issues that relate to external constituencies. He may be assertive in style, but he is solicitous of the individualized approach to academic functions and usually devotes considerable attention to the amorphous pursuit of caring for faculty. Administration must have a personal quality. If an administrator concludes that the situation is sufficiently critical to preclude his using time so lavishly, then he should count on resistance from his faculty colleagues.

Having identified the limits within which he can operate without running afoul of the academic perception, the administrator must next determine the guiding principles of discourse that correspond to the highly individualized spirit of the academician. The implications of the academic perception for administration are sometimes difficult for administrators to grasp, even those who have themselves been members of the faculty. But this need not be. Successful relations with faculty begin with the understanding that nothing may be so important as the willingness to express approval over what others are doing. The individual search for approbation which we see on the part of all people in all kinds of social situations is particularly strong among academicians. As a member of a lonely profession that relates poorly to institutions, the academician experiences little reinforcement for his acts from his routine working relationships. Academia does not have the support system of bureaucratic organization. Because a university's employees do not work in an interdependent fashion, the academician will not necessarily be sustained by those around him simply because he practices "positive organizational behavior."

Any approval that comes the academician's way is important to him only if it expresses recognition of personal accomplishments rather than group achievements. For long periods, nothing may occur to solicit this approval. Yet, the formalities of institutional approbation are an important motivating force. Ideally, only those bureaucratic decisions that convey approval of individual requests are transmitted directly to the academician. If a denial is necessary, the message should be less direct. Preliminary exploration of a tentative request from an individual faculty member is useful to determine whether approval can be forthcoming. If not, then a formal request from the academician is usually not advisable, and some way should be found to forestall it. A little disappointment at this juncture is preferable to rejection later on.

The academician's desire for personal approbation can also relate to budget procedures. Customarily, monies are allocated to departments on the basis of a justification submitted annually by the department as a group. Nevertheless, many administrators retain discretionary funds in accounts for supplies, equipment, student help, and honoraria, which they dole out individually to faculty members as the occasion arises. This practice does not mean an administrator is being patronizing or savoring power over the academician. It is simply a device for expressing institutional approval, and that approval is most explicit when the individual academician is requesting something for his work that is distinct from the activities of colleagues in his department. Often the request is for such a small amount that the administrator can be mystified over why it was made in the first place. The magnitude of the request is not the point. More often it is a matter of the academician's being afforded an opportunity for approbation.

Administrators cannot always maintain the personal quality in their official stance. Emphasizing personal relationships requires an inordinate amount of time. It means almost constant availability to faculty. For the administrator who is obsessed with orderliness or formality, this approach is particularly difficult because a precise daily schedule can become a shambles. A dean's office is thereby reduced to the stall of an Arab rug merchant who transacts business simultaneously with three or more customers. Yet, it may be well to remember that it is the academician, not the administrator, who creates the product of the university, often in a way that is quite independent of the academic dean or vice-president. Thus, the expression of approbation—the caring for people—may be one of the more worthwhile functions performed by an administrator from the standpoint of the quality of a university's program.

One of the impacts of collective bargaining in academic relationships is seen in the requirement under contracts that administrators inform candidates for promotion, tenure, and renewal of any negative recommendations on their part. However artfully these statements may be worded, when such letters go to 10 percent of faculty (the proportion that may apply but are not recommended for promotion), a dean's relations with faculty suffer a severe jolt. And this is a yearly occurrence. Any negative response from the administration on these matters can be seen by the individual academician only as total and personal rejection. He cannot accept the explanation that the outcome serves the interests of the university. How can institutional interests ever be placed above those of the independent practitioner? Nor can the academician really understand interpretations based on a limited number of dollars for promotion or the necessity of administrators to make relative judgments—comparing one candidate with another and recommending only the more worthy. Both ideas are alien to the academic perception. A very large part of the academician's performance depends on continuing self-esteem, and often administrators are put in positions from which they cannot help sustain it.

The rise of faculty unionism also brings the occasion for increased litigation over a university's decisions, particularly as they apply to a profession that is inclined to argue each case on its merits. As a protective device, administrators are now being advised by counsel to be more cautious in affording approbation in normal correspondence with faculty members. Otherwise, past indications of approval may be used as evidence in grievance hearings and court cases by disappointed candidates for promotion and renewal. The message expressing approbation is then cited by the litigant as being inconsistent with the administrator's subsequent decision. Because it was misleading, so the plaintiff argues, it justifies a reversal of that decision. Apparently, on some campuses, the situation has reached a point where even the phrase "high professional esteem" is no longer used in the complimentary close of letters, particularly in those informing an untenured faculty member that his contract has not been renewed. Who can say when even this formal expression of approbation associated more with civility than with commendation might become evidence in legal proceedings? This entire development is much more injurious than many would believe because administrative (and therefore university) approval of the individual academician's activities is much more important than most realize. One of the few supportive devices that a university can use in its relations with the independent entrepreneur is now being denied it.

5

The Academic Political Paradigm

The political ideal of academia is to be found in Robert Wolff's rational community. This vision embodies direct participation by all of its members in deliberations that determine the social milieu. There is reciprocity among participants. Each is made aware of the other as the result of public discourse among equals. The proceedings are not simply instrumental. They have intrinsic worth, and participants work toward political order through the essence of dialogue. Wolff has his rational community rise above the goals of liberal democracy. Its purpose is not simply to provide a sense of justice in the distribution of the fruits of society while permitting the individual to pursue private interests. The ideal society collectively cherishes its culture and traditions. It engages in enterprises that are enjoyed not simply for what they might produce but also for themselves.[1]

In his description of a rationalist, Michael Oakeshott has provided an archetype of the citizen who resides in the academic community. Oakeshott's rationalist is independent of mind. His thought is free from obligation to any authority other than reason. He believes that reason is common to all persons, who are capable of judging all phenomena. If this rational creature appears sometimes to ignore the experience of others in reaching his decisions, it is only because he insists on verifying everything himself: all experience must be his own.[2] As a Cartesian, his mind is his only guide in the pursuit of knowledge, which in turn determines action.

David Braybooke and Charles E. Lindbloom complete our model of academia with a concept of social action that fits the structure and participants of the rational community. Characterized as a rational and deductive ideal for decision making, the process involves principles—

intuitive notions of goodness—derived from experience. Reason dictates that for experience to be useful within some sense of social continuity, it must be reduced to a set of principles. These principles are set into an ethical system and arranged so as to indicate which tenets govern the application of all other rules of conduct. The principles are broad enough to cover a variety of propositions from which solutions to specific problems can be found. An outcome or a conclusion in any instance is deduced by logic based on fact and hypothesis.[3] To provide perspective for their logical culture, Braybooke and Lindbloom contrast it to American liberal pluralism, which operates according to group or individual preference with neither values nor ends being stated explicitly.[4]

Rational Politics

The political culture of academia incorporates the features of organization, individual perception, and process found in this rational paradigm. Wolff's politics of dialogue call for direct participation, small group relationships, and coalescence around values rather than through common interests. Oakeshott's rationalist has the outlook Descartes identified with an individual seeking the cultivation of his own reason. Our community member relies on personal observation, approaches action independently, strives for rational solution, and recognizes no limitation on the application of reason. The rational and deductive ideal of Braybooke and Lindbloom rests on the individualistic, value-oriented, and principle-producing type of decision making that fits the structure and performance of the academic political process. The academician attempts to treat even his own experience objectively by reducing it to principles for governing professional conduct.

Within the academic context, the politics of rational dialogue substitutes individual expression and the rational decisions of a collegium for appeals to higher authority found in the juridical and bureaucratic aspects of open society. It thereby allows for the dispersing of power and responsibility, a practice already noted to be prevalent in academic organization. To the extent that power perseveres, it is in rational argument—the weapon of the individual.

As rationalists, academicians also demonstrate a proclivity for the universals of comprehensive solution. The process by which an issue is resolved must have a quality of completeness. There must first be a statement of principles. Then all aspects of the situation are illuminated with facts. The incremental and incomplete solutions that characterize pluralistic politics are seen as nothing more than removing the issue temporarily from the agenda. In the final analysis, this approach is dismissed as a waste of time. The rationalist's technique for reaching decisions does, of course, have pitfalls. Proposed solutions tend to embody the ideal, and academic rationalists find themselves bearing the frustration of grappling with a reality that inadequately embodies it. Nevertheless, because of the compulsion to approach problems rationally, the command of all facts distinguishes academic decision-making.

This proposition can easily be tested. If a participant in academic decision making confronts the group with a new fact at the very moment of decision, chances are that action will be delayed until the information can be worked into the rational and inclusive construct that governs action. For the same reason, action can also be suspended in academic proceedings by suggesting the existence of data that may have a bearing on the situation but, for the time being, are not readily available. Under these conditions the academician cannot proceed insofar as action must be based on rational consideration of all information. Great frustration will be experienced by those who are involved while a frantic search for the facts is initiated.

Rational decision making and its concomitant, the holistic approach to problem solving, can also be observed in the difficulty academicians have in limiting themselves to an assigned mission. Anything even remotely related to the topic at hand receives consideration. There is no clear distinction between an assembly giving legitimacy to a proposal that has been reached through the arduous work of others and one that examines a matter from its inception. Anyone familiar with academic politics is aware of the perplexity a faculty senate encounters in a proposal prepared for it by a committee of its members. A simple vote on the measure, perhaps after minor amendment, seldom occurs. Invariably, the entire body wants to act as its own drafting committee.

The academician's insistence on rationality, combined with his compulsion to seek the whole of any situation, has profound implications for the politics of a university. The first of these that might be noted is the efficacy of dialogue. As a means of glorifying principles, dialogue gives academic politics an obvious ingredient—proceedings have an unending quality about them. Contrary to the practice of politics in our broader society, free expression is not for the purpose of assuring that all legitimate interests are involved in the political process. Dialogue is meant to impart knowledge as the closed group of intellectuals works toward a rational solution. Talk becomes the essence of politics. As Wolff has suggested, it has social value for participants. It embodies expression for its own sake, a means of articulation that easily lends itself to the academician's penchant for symbolism.

In examining a political matter, faculty seldom take the shortest route to a solution that is "politic" or fruitful. Every possible course and recourse must not only be indicated, but must be fully explored as well. Many propositions are little more than exercises in mental agility. Proposals are advanced almost hypothetically, independent of any thought of moving proceedings along. Malformed mutations abound. Talk is cheap, and in governance assemblies there is plenty of it. The lengthy proceedings of such bodies and the intensity of debate can be misleading from the standpoint of their bearing on a political outcome. Actually, the nature and extent of discussion may be illustrative of little more than a popular academic art form.

Another feature of academic politics is that the tendency to seek rational decisions derived from a set of principles sometimes works against compromise. Programs and proposals are often measured by their consistency with values rather than their effectiveness in achieving some group goal. As a result, compromise (a standard political technique for resolving problems) is seen as an attack on principles and the solutions they are meant to achieve. Consequently, compromise is not always applauded by individual faculty members. In fact, it can be loathsome. The reason, of course, is not difficult to find. For the academician pursuing his independent and holistic ways, organization preferably remains a vague form. Consequently, little value is given to those factors, such as compromise, which sustain organization. Academicians have other ways of achieving harmony within their community. In the academic setting, neither organization nor group decision embodies the power to command submission in the same way as for those who work under bureaucratic conditions.

A third characteristic that rationality gives academic politics has already been noted. Whenever a new political circumstance (or fact) is introduced, it must be worked into the rational system of abstract principles that is meant to govern action. A set of facts, not political power or individual and subgroup interests, is intended to determine outcome. But something that has not been noted is the impact this practice has on academic decision making. Any decision taken in the past need not guide the future. In the face of today's evidence and the principles it produces, yesterday's decisions have low powers of commitment. The end result is that in their decision making, academicians seem to have no memory, and the process of formulating principles sometimes takes on greater importance than arriving at a solution that can serve the purpose of continuity. The college catalog may be cited by an academic politician as a compendium of rules and regulations which all are expected to follow slavishly—particularly deans. But once the decision-making process is initiated, anything can be changed if reason alone so dictates. The academic political process, therefore, tends to be unending, uncompromising, and unpredictable.

The Problem of Pluralistic Concepts

These qualities place their mark on academic politics. They produce a system having assumptions that often do not fit with those of our society's pluralistic practices. A basic assumption of pluralism is that all Americans accept representative and legislative deliberative bodies and are comfortable with them. This prescription does not always hold for the academician, even while he is being called upon to participate in the governing bodies of his college or university. When a faculty member is placed within a representational legislative context and asked to make or to modify educational polity, the first question to arise for him is whether one academician can truly represent another. After all, if politics are pursued in terms of rational discourse, and if reason is the tool of the individual, then every individual must have a voice in any decision taken by the group.

Collegiality requires, therefore, that legitimate acts be identified with the participation of all members of the collegium. Action is not determined by a vote in the ordinary sense; it is the outcome of an emerging consensus that may be formalized by a vote. Representation denies most members their collegial right to speak; and on matters of academic policy, one individual cannot commit another. Thus, the issue goes beyond the question of representation for other constituencies of the university. It raises the problem of how academicians themselves relate to one another in a representative decision-making process. Representative governance systems have, of course, been instituted at most campuses, principally because faculties have become so large that a general convention of faculty would be unwieldy. But because of faculty perceptions, there is an inclination to fashion commissions, councils, or senates as much for the purposes of furthering dialogue as for legislating for the community.

Even after legislative action is taken, faculty acquiescence must be gained. The vote of a senate or curriculum committee does not necessarily achieve this purpose. As a proposal works its way through the governance system, faculty exposure increases and rational arguments are marshaled. An inordinate number of gatherings at which the legislation is considered may be necessary before those responsible for program execution feel free to proceed. A plan may have received approval "in principle" from governance bodies months before, but it is still necessary to convince the independent-minded academician who did not take part in these deliberations of the merits of the proposal. Within the academic culture, political discourse has intrinsic value because it sustains community. Everyone must participate. Implementation of a proposal does not ensue from enactment. It is the result of a meeting of minds occurring as a result of the more lengthy process of full discussion within the community.

Many academicians harbor a suspicion of universitywide governance, partially because of the dualism they see it bringing to academic structure. Few faculty members identify with university committees and councils to the same extent that they identify with their departments, where political unity is reinforced by professional mutualities. Even when the academician represents his department on a committee or deliberative body, he often sees the proceedings as detracting from the efficacy of his discipline. In his view, whatever decisions are taken could limit the actions of the department and the freedom of the academician, who would otherwise be content operating within the conventions of his discipline.

The findings of Dressel and his associates in their survey of faculty attitudes reflected this view of universitywide governance. Faculty saw an inverse relationship between the influence of departments and that of the administration. The influence of the administration and that of university committees, however, was directly related.[5] Faculty believe administrators and students achieve power and influence through university committees, even though many academicians are not willing to take up the cudgels of pluralistic practice to challenge other constituencies for the power found in such bodies.

I achieved the same results as Dressel in a survey conducted at Colgate University in 1973. From a faculty of about 175, 46 persons were identified as "opinion leaders" on the basis of membership on policy-making bodies over the previous six years. These were the same people who attended and took an active role in the meetings of the corporate faculty. From this group, 42 were available for interviews. On questions pertaining to governance, 23 contended that representation was not a legitimate function in the collegial organization to which they aspired at Colgate. In common with the respondents to the Dressel survey, 28 concluded that a university council consisting of faculty, students, and administrators does not serve all constituencies equally well. From those who held this view, 21 believed that the interests of the administrators were best served, although there were only 4 administrative members and 8 student members on the university council as opposed to 16 faculty members. Despite the faculty's numerical advantage, none saw faculty interests as being best served by the body. An even greater number (35) held that faculty should never be committed to a change of educational policy by a majority vote of the council.

The complexities of academic governance were revealed in the circumstance of the survey. Colgate's multiconstituency council had been established with overwhelming support from the faculty, including these same opinion leaders, just three years earlier. Yet, even the opinion leaders (those faculty who were active and respected in the affairs of the college), were dissatisfied with governance. Twice as many (22) saw governance and quasi-administration to be a serious problem associated with working at Colgate as any other disadvantage. Other undesirable features of the university were listed as insufficient opportunities for outside professional contact (11), administrative manipulation of faculty (8), limitations of the library (7), too heavy a teaching load (5), and insufficient research funds (4). Only two respondents included low salaries among adverse aspects of an association with Colgate.

In 1975, faculty at Stockton State College of New Jersey, an institution noted by David Riesman in his work,[6] showed much the same scorn for governance. In an effort to establish a college council at this new and innovative institution, the vice-president for academic affairs asked individual faculty members to seek nomination for elections to the college council by submitting a petition of candidacy that included the signature of peers. Only 8 of 130 faculty bothered to do so. Yet, the faculty continued to demand greater consultation with administrators in the operation of the college. A college council was obviously not seen as an appropriate body for achieving what the faculty considered to be true consultation. A greater role for departments (which had not been fully recognized) and an outcome in administrative decisions that reflected more of the academic perception were the principal objectives of the faculty. Particularly with regard to the latter, the faculty felt that their views were not being considered.

Even though an academician questions the validity of representational bodies, because representation now exists in academic politics, he is likely to find himself a member of one or more university committees. Placed in this situation, how does he respond to the demands of parliamentary technique—processing and aggregating interests, taking positions through a vote, and being guided by standard procedures? Faculty do not necessarily consider academia to be an open polity. As a result, the issue of governance is not to determine majority preference with its assumptions of equality. The thought of a delegate's being elected to a rule-making body where his success and longevity are determined by how well he represents the interests of constituents becomes a questionable proposition. The academician may consider his position a chore, not a privilege, and thus be thankful when the day arrives for him to relinquish his office. On the other hand, the maneuverability implied for the individual constituent to shift allegiance from one representative to another as he reinterprets his interests at election time does not reflect academic reality, either.

The academician's interpretation of the role of a faculty member serving on a university council is reminiscent of Weber's "free representative" who is not bound by pressures from constituents. He is obligated to express his genuine conviction but not to promote the interests of those who elect him.[7] Faculty often refer to this approach as the Burkean concept of representation. Two hundred years ago, Edmund Burke contended that a representative in a deliberative body must rely on his own "unbiased opinion, his mature judgment and his enlightened conscience." Burke characterized these attributes as a "trust of Providence." Regarding the relationship between the constituent and his representative, Burke inveighed against "authoritative instructions to the representative, mandates issued, which a member is bound blindly and implicitly to obey, to vote, and to argue for, though contrary to the clear conviction of his judgment and his conscience." Government and legislation, Burke contended, are matters of reason, not of personal will and inclination.[8] Like Burke, the academician claims to vote according to his conscience rather than to represent a constituency.

The representative function is perhaps the most obvious aspect of politics upon which contrasts can be drawn between our pluralistic and the academic society. With regard to other features of a political system, it may be useful to cite the assumptions of contemporary pluralism and decide how well these apply to academia. In his exploration of American democracy, Robert Dahl begins with James Madison's perception of political factions being formed and operating in accordance with personal interests their respective members hold in common. Madison's concern was to find a means of controlling conflict between the majority and the minority. Power is managed, he reasoned, by maintaining that it is derived from the people as a whole; domination of power by a majority faction is prevented if the electorate is numerous, extended, and diverse in its interests. If interests are varied, coalitions will be unstable, any majority faction will be transitory, and a permanent majority that would be tempted to develop authoritarian proclivities can be avoided.[9]

Theodore Lowi adds both an economic and an organizational dimension to the American system with his observation that the driving force of our society is found in its division of labor, its massive production of wealth, and the techniques it has evolved for distributing that wealth. For the purposes of this argument, these concepts need not be developed or their relationships explored. It is sufficient to note that the egalitarian, competitive, and interest-group orientations of American political life are enough to focus attention on essentially materialistic concerns. Lowi elaborates on Madison's conflict-control theme by pointing out that power is manifest in intergroup bargaining. The dominant feature of our current system, as he sees it, is organization—an administrative core that permits an interest group to perpetuate itself through a hierarchy capable of articulating group goals, integrating members, and exerting influence.[10]

Finally, William E. Connolly completes the system with the concept of aggregation and discrete government. Interest groups are fluid. Each individual has a number of interests, and the system provides alternative power centers through which he can influence various aspects of policy. Generally, interest groups work through parties that attempt to accommodate a variety of interests in order to maintain a winning coalition. Government becomes an arena in which political parties, each representing a conglomeration of interests, attempt to shape political outcome. To a growing extent, however, government is also an umpire that assures equity among the interest groups. In responding to and adjudicating among special interests, the government supposedly ensures the public interest.[11]

Conceptually, the holistic, independent, and ascriptive norms of the academician are contradictory to almost every aspect of the differentiated, interdependent, and impersonal standards applied in these political features of our pluralistic society. In academia, power is not derived from the people. It springs from intellect. In fact, the very legitimacy of power is questioned by the academician insofar as power implies a concentration of influence that is used to determine the distribution of resources. Having no need for rampant power in his individual and holistic Cartesian pursuits, the academician has no use for those societal structures that channel and control it or that mediate among groups during conflict in contention over limited resources.

Within open society, governing systems strive for effectiveness in maintaining the power and marshaling the resources necessary to achieve the goals announced for the collective by its leadership. An academician is more likely to see governance as assembly for purposes of rational expression leading to internal harmony. Goals enunciated by an institutional leader are almost automatically suspect. The academician experiences no division of labor, has no clear concept of scarcity, and finds talk of productivity anathema to his thinking. He sees scholarship as an effort to express values. Consequently, it is a qualitative, not a quantitative pursuit. Competition connotes efficiency based on comparative judgments. It may be a potent incentive when rewards are allocated on the basis of performance. In academia, however, comparisons among disciplines for the purpose of resource allocation cannot be made. Each discipline determines its own excellence.

Finally, the concept of interest itself is not acceptable to the academician. The thought of interest group pitted against interest group is viewed as being destructive to genuine community. One of the more fascinating expressions of academic thinking on governance is found in the 1968 report of the Berkeley Study Commission on University Governance. The students and faculty who prepared the report rejected "interest group pluralism" with its commitment to bargaining. They saw it as imposing unjustifiably narrow limits on the process of academic discussion and decision making.[12]

The Conservative Bias

One of the more provocative conclusions to emerge from this review of academic politics may be that with regard to his profession and how it is conducted, the academician is a conservative fellow. Admittedly, political action of any type is premised on the achievement of some goal, which in itself incorporates the idea of progress. The rational politics of the academician are no different in this respect. They, too, have a concept of progress. Rationality, in fact, creates a sense of the imperative which equates the unethical with a failure to proceed with whatever reason requires. In Oakeshott's extreme formulation of rationality at work, nothing stands in the way of a society's meeting its felt needs. As the author of his own acts, the rationalist claims influence over his destiny. For a community imbued with the concept of progress occurring through rational problem solving, politics can become a series of crises in which intense energy is brought to bear in disposing of each succeeding impediment to the achievement of an ever-expanding concept of need.[13] This interpretation of rationalism suggests that intellect itself, through its powers of definition, creates needs and problems as well as solutions. It is an approach that explains the academic practice of program and course proliferation within the curriculum of a college. A constantly expanding universe of intellectual concern is necessary for the academician's sense of well-being. A concept of progress is clearly present.

Nevertheless, a static element does prevail within a university setting. The essence of progress is not always dramatic. It may be as Oakeshott implies: at the heart of rational politics is the concept of the superiority of the unencumbered intellect. And for the academician nothing is more important than to assure that the intellect remains unencumbered. This corollary immediately places restraints on progress. All novelty must be structured so as not to conflict with the preservation of two Cartesian principles—freedom for the individual who seeks to develop his reason and assurance of the stability and security necessary for intellectual pursuits. Almost miraculously, when the burdens of adjustment to institutional change are to be shouldered, the academician will see to it that the student assumes the task in adapting to new requirements or the administrator takes on responsibility for devising new procedures and instituting new practices for whatever innovation the fertile academic imagination might have developed. Normally, in any faculty-initiated proposal for change, classroom performance remains unaltered. The sanctity of academic time is respected.

Somewhat contradictory to Oakeshott's proposition, the academician abhors crisis because it is detrimental to the stability he requires for intellectual activities. Nevertheless, the sense of crisis experienced by Oakeshott's rationalist may still be present in the academician's politics. But this sense of crisis is intellectual; it need not alter physical conditions. As a result, it is not destabilizing for our rationalist. It is compatible with an academician's intellectual pursuits. All other conditions must remain stable as he struggles with some issue of the mind. Essentially, the so-called crisis is invigorating. It does not threaten. Consequently, the academician can show objectivity in his considerations. Here we see the detachment expressed in the fourth Cartesian principle. The academician need not become embroiled in political action. He is skilled, it would seem, only in applying rational solutions to the situations of others. In the final analysis, academic politics are more rationalistic in form than rational in content.

The prevailing view in our society is that colleges are bastions of liberal thought and formulation because academicians are generally of a liberal outlook. But the academician encounters a series of snares and traps that make life uncomfortable without his often being fully aware of the source of the difficulty. The problem arises because he lives in a society guided by pluralistic concepts yet he works in the world of academic exclusivity. He is subject to the influence of two standards. He is sometimes ambivalent, therefore, about such societal conceptions as progress and its handmaid, equality. Usually he will agree "in principle" to the efficacy of either concept as a guiding proposition for society. Even with regard to the university, he may see both as being applicable. He may not take exception, for example, when the idea of progress is invoked as justification for a change in the educational program to introduce such practices as team teaching of core courses, which, incidentally, militates against independent performance. Likewise, he may find equality a good reason for permitting students or middle-level administrators representing student affairs and the registrar's and admissions offices to share his authoritative role in the senate where the university determines educational policy. In fact, new approaches to program or governance are often acceptable to that element of his consciousness associated with open society.

Faculty assent does not mean, however, that the academician is about to surrender either those institutional symbols that solemnize independent performance or those faculty prerogatives that apply to educational policy. At the time of the implementation of a new program, a substantial amount of tension can arise over attempts by administrators to operate under rules the academician has previously accepted in principle. At this point, having satisfied his societal sense of equality and program, he reverts to his academic image. A more defensive posture is natural because it is now an administrator who becomes the actor. Whereas no danger to the academic mission oc-cured in the affirmation of generally accepted beliefs—a symbolic act in itself—a threat can be perceived in the implementation of programs that embody these same beliefs. The academician's outlook is now much more conservative.

In a college senate that includes representatives of nonfaculty constituencies, a question will arise regarding the propriety of allowing other than faculty to vote on certain curricular matters. The same question is debated when the senate is vested under collective bargain-ing agreements with responsibility for electing working conditions committees. To begin with, the faculty's sense of being the university causes the academician to insist that such matters be formalized by a collegial senate. Thereupon faculty are confronted by the voting pre-rogatives of other constituencies that are also represented in the senate. Invariably, the suggestion will arise that only "certain senators" be permitted to vote in the elections for the working conditions com-mittee. In such cases, faculty exclusivity clashes with the equally lively idea championed by other constituents who have concern for the "whole university." In their failure to consider faculty ambivalence on issues of progress, administrators are often caught unaware by the violent reaction of academicians to seemingly straightforward efforts at strengthening a university's image with new programs and systems of governance. Under these circumstances, rules may have been changed, but the old doctrines have remained intact.

For an interpretation of academia, Edmund Burke provides more than just the idea of representation. Burke's world is also compatible with the academician's stability and harmony insofar as he advocates "peace, quiet, and security of the realm" for which constituent parts are obliged to hold public faith with one another. "Otherwise competence and power will soon be confounded and no law will be left but the will of a prevailing force." In a university setting, competence and power are embedded in academic mission, whereas force is equated with the university's management. For Burke, the norms of a political culture are determined by a "reference to antiquity," and anything that disturbs them is viewed with utmost suspicion. In fact, "a spirit of innovation is generally the result of a selfish temper and confined view." Here, too, is the response of the academician when presented with many of the changes that have been pressed on universities in recent years.

Representative and legislative proceedings in the name of a larger institution can be an embarrassment for someone who, like Burke, sees identity and security in his own special "little platoon," a perfect analogy to the academic department. In Burke's terms, "We entertain a high opinion of the legislative authority; but we have never dreamt that parliament had any right whatever…to override prescription." The notion of there being a "representative public" is defined in Burke's assertion, "And I see as little of policy or utility as there is of right, in laying down a principle that a majority of men told by its head are to be considered as the people, and that as such their will is to be law."

Thus the torment of pluralism for the academician, when he is confronted by authoritative dicta from students and outside managers, can be paraphrased in the traditional language of conservatism. The classic academician can be very much at home with Burke's observation about interest group politics—"what sort of reason is that in which the determination precedes the discussion?" What Cartesian in professing the academic culture would not agree with Burke that "the pride of the human intellect…is the collected reason of ages"?[14] The academic prescription is neatly conservative.

The Academician's Dissatisfaction

Despite the serenity that the academician seeks in a stable and essentially conservative environment, his politics can be the source of considerable dissatisfaction for him. Dissonance derives, in fact, from fashioning a community premised on rational dialogue. One of the contradictions this perception brings to academic politics is that the style of academic performance does not always allow rational consideration (as based on the efficacy of dialogue) to result in a strong sense of community. The individual preferences of the professors and the principles that guide them are often considered more important than the community itself. The individual's performance can be perceived as being separate from the university. Consequently, the outcome Robert Wolff saw from the affective relationships of the rational community—the collective cherishing of its culture and traditions—does not always materialize in the behavior of the academician. It remains elusive, largely because of the academician's independence, even while faculty venerate the small group. In this situation we see the basis of Thibaut and Kelley's observation that groups distinguished by self-oriented behavior experience a low sense of satisfaction from or interest in group endeavors. The sense of personal fulfillment in community is never realized.

One explanation of the difficulties encountered in academic politics suggests that although rational dialogue may occur, it does not always conclude in a well-reasoned outcome. The academician is depicted in this formulation as an expert in making distinctions. He is someone, it has been said, who thinks otherwise. His art is one of revealing inconsistencies and contradictions rather than working toward agreement. It all fits with a high level of individual expression and rationality in problem solving. But in the process of constantly making distinctions, the academician loses political effectiveness—the ability to coalesce— and with it whatever satisfaction political resolution might bring.

In a culture in which dialogue has such great importance, the supposition is easily made that an individual has the right to say anything as long as it is not unethical. Here we encounter a serious problem for our rational community. The propriety of virtually unlimited expression seems consistent with the veneration given academic freedom. It is strengthened by the knowledge that no one in academe suffers sanctions from political parlance. Reputation and performance are assessed on the basis of scholarly work and teaching, not by standards of political conduct. Some academicians see no danger in a little political intemperance or in the inclination within many faculties to engage in mutual vilification. In fact, tolerance is an item that is often in noticeably short supply in college politics. In the academician's performance as a teacher and scholar, the low level of tolerance is not always apparent because of the independent and holistic fashion in which he works. Interaction often is not required. Consequently, tolerance is not an issue. But we may be sure that the expressions of intolerance that are present in a university lead to dissatisfaction in the business of politics, even among those who appear to relish university governance as a pastime.

Even parliamentary procedure operates against the academician's perception of decision making. The practice of disposing first of amendments and substitute motions, for example, gives priority in discussion to deviations from the basic idea that is under consideration. If in academic political procedures, deliberations are more expressive than instrumental, then Robert's Rules of Order have a disconcerting influence. They center attention on what many consider the undesirable or peripheral features of a legislative item. In approaching a vote, the academician may find the underlying concept of the proposal acceptable. But as compromises among competing views are hammered out, many of the ideas put forward as amendments can violate the essential theme of the original proposal. Each participant in the proceedings has his own view of unity and consistency. Some may believe that a critical aspect of the original concept has been mutilated by amendments or procedures associated with implementation. In such cases, it is not uncommon for an academician to vote against a proposal he had vigorously supported at the outset.

Actually such votes often have little to do with the interests of the voting parliamentarian. Shifts in a representative's position often appear erratic, even when consistency in voting records exists. Continuity is to be found in an individual's interpretation of principle, not in blocks or associations of representatives accommodating one another's interests through trade-offs. To the extent that coalitions can be discerned, they are negative and transitory, encompassing a variety of principles that dictate opposition to a piece of legislation. Surely there are instances in which the faculty as a whole sees a corporate grievance, and these provide an occasion for coalescence and heightened participation. But because such situations usually emphasize the coming together in opposition to some action (usually a proposal from other constituents of the university), they do not involve persevering aspects of faculty behavior. When the threat recedes, so does the unity. The solidarity that such occasions effect is soon attenuated, leaving the same community of loosely knit and independently functioning individual academicians.

By turning again to the wisdom of F. M. Cornford we will acquire added insight into the dissatisfaction of the academician. To achieve their ends, Cornford concluded, academicians had vested sovereign authority in a senate, which he saw as a body without corporate feeling, "being necessarily ignorant of the decisive considerations in almost all the business submitted to it." The dangers encountered in the occasional sense of responsibility that might be experienced by an individual faculty member is minimized, Cornford observed, by "not allowing anyone to act without first consulting at least twenty other people who are accustomed to regard him with well-founded suspicion....Twenty independent persons, each of whom has a different reason for not doing a certain thing, and no one of whom will compromise with the other, constitute a most effective check upon the rashness of individuals."

Cornford aptly summarized the situation in his allusions to parliamentary practice: "As soon as three or more alternatives are in the field, there is pretty sure to be a majority against anyone of them and nothing will be done. The method of *Prevarication* is based upon a very characteristic trait of the academic mind, which comes out in the common remark, 'I was in favor of the proposal until I heard Mr. ____'s argument in support of it.' The principle is that a few bad reasons for doing something neutralise all the good reasons for doing it. Since this is devoutly believed, it is often the best policy to argue weakly against the side you favor."[15] Should there be any wonder that this type of politics breeds dissatisfaction?

A moderating influence attributed to the American scene that often softens disputes and ameliorates dissatisfaction in politics is the acceptance of laws as rules of conduct and the belief that authority in a society of equals can govern with these laws. The tradition of our pluralistic system is that after the polemics, interest groups are willing to settle for a set of rules and to play by them, perhaps with just a little subversion from time to time. The political process centers on the manipulation of these rules (within certain bounds) to achieve one's objectives. But a difference exists between academia and pluralism on the matter of rules versus principles, and this difference is important to the operation of a university. Judith Shklar has characterized it as the difference between the moral decisionist and the legal theorist. Although Shklar was not writing about academia, she identifies the moral decisionist with "academic reality." He has no need for a rule book, whether it be a book of convention, ideology, or institutional relationships. As the lone decider, working from his ascriptively assigned position, the moral decisionist has the right to judge. Facts and rational judgment are sufficient for reaching a decision in the face of any situation. Rules, in fact, become unreal symbols that can distort the decisionist's purpose. The calculations of reason serve reality.[16] Here we encounter the full force of Descartes's third axiom—"I was assured of using my reason in everything."

What administrator has not experienced the faculty member who commits funds by inviting an important speaker to campus without prior approval on the assumption that funds will be available simply because they have been in the past. And there is the chairman who orders equipment and supplies by telephone when the university's procedures require prior authorization for such orders from a number of administrative offices. Grading regulations—changing grades, removing incompletes, observing deadlines for withdrawals, and the like—become a shambles as faculty approach requests from students individually without regard for the grading system and the equity it is meant to provide for all students. In each case, the academician defends his position with the assertion that he is being reasonable. The course must be enriched by the outside speaker; the supplies must be acquired immediately if laboratories are to be stocked; a student should not be held to arbitrary practices that have little to do with learning. The moral decision of academic reality is at work when academicians take such actions independent of the procedures of the university.

Shklar's description, is, of course, that of the individual released from the controls of social structure. Such thinking—reason over rules—is at the foundations of academia with its insistence on independent, holistic, and ascriptive performance guided by abstract principles. If there is no need for rules in academia, then there is no need for the power to enforce them or the structure to transmit signals regarding their application. The entrepreneurial nature of the academician's style of performance goes a long way toward explaining his view of administrative functions, institutional responsibility, organizational structure, and the rules all these engender. The moral decisionist believes he has little need for an institution to achieve his ends. Reason is enough. Thus, we can see the core of the academician's resistance to organization, even at a time when the drive for "effectiveness" in our society requires each interest group and profession to permit personal considerations to become contingent upon the purposes of the organization that gives participants identity. The unfortunate part of the political formulations of the moral decisionist is that they lead to conflict with the concepts of institution. And conflict is a source of dissatisfaction for the academician in his search for stability.

Governing the Academy

How, then, can academia be governed? Clark Kerr has suggested a United Nations model—several nations, each with its territory, jurisdiction, and form of government; each having the ability to declare war; and some having the power of veto. In such a society of multiple cultures, he concludes, coexistence is more likely than unity.[17] Kerr's approach reflects the theoretical autocephalous underpinnings of the university. It has the virtue of emphasizing the futility of attempting to work within a pluralistic framework that attempts to achieve a limited harmony by somehow aggregating constituent interests.

Left to their own devices, many academicians favor the division of authority implied by Kerr. In fact, the successful sharing of common responsibilities within the academic state has become increasingly less popular over the years. Lewis B. Mayhew and, to an extent, Howard R. Bowen propose an allocation of powers among a university's constituents by which students, administrators, and faculty are each vested with a special competence in certain areas of the university's life. Within reason, others accept whatever that group decides.[18] This system permits one group to encounter the other in a functional but not in a political sense, and contention is thereby minimized. This is the way of the academician's harmony.

Ideally, academicians still see the logic of an unicameral multiconstituent legislative body. They are, after all, still members of a society that is dedicated to pluralism. They often acknowledge that a separate student government is an inadequate means of assuring student participation in the formulation of university policies and programs. Yet, there is an inclination to preserve for the faculty all initiative in educational policy. The proposal of Mayhew and Bowen as well as the image drawn by Kerr serve this purpose.

Behind every proposal for governance devised by an academician is the element of faculty exclusivity. The difficulty in settling on a system—in fact, the dissatisfaction with most governance proceedings—stems from the differences among constituents over faculty prerogatives. Will the curriculum serve the narrow interests of the academic discipline and leave the academician's time untaxed by demands beyond his own intellectual concerns? Or will it also reflect some institutional feature which the administrators can claim is unique and of which they can be proud? Simultaneously, will it accommodate the public by devoting major attention to the latest demands from the marketplace, such as programs of business administration and a myriad of middle-level practical technologies that previously were not associated with a college degree?

The faculty is distinguished from other constituents of the university in that the faculty alone is committed to teaching and academic discipline. These are symbols, from which the academician derives a sense of mission that gives him special powers. The quality of exclusiveness is embodied in this commitment. Particularly if a group feels threatened, it may attempt to enhance its power by idealizing its functions, giving its endeavors moral sanction, and endowing itself with a superior office. Faculty members are no exception. Academic mission, in fact, is the complement of the academician's major symbol, faculty as university.

Although faculty recognize the necessity to take part in a university's decisions, academicians often prefer informal consultation to involvement through a formal structure. Power, politics, and the contention of a division formalized by a vote need not be a part of such deliberations. Some academicians will suggest, therefore, that if multiconstituent representation is necessary, it should be in a president's council having advisory functions and vague prerogatives for reviewing educational philosophy. Simultaneously, the faculty would exercise exclusive authority over curriculum. In this model, there is little assurance that the faculty's curricular mores would correspond with the pluralism of notions that the outside constituencies would be inclined to express in council sessions. The problem posed by such a system is whether it can persist if its principles, as fashioned by academicians, are at variance with the rule-making inclination of pluralists. Under such a system, the suspicion naturally grows that one constituency or another might not take the deliberations of the advisory council seriously. Faculty, in particular, would proceed with their work whatever the views of the council.

But, if circumvention is likely, a new question arises: How can the academician's desire for exclusivity be made compatible with the public's demands for participation in the making of academic decisions? But the academician's answer does not change. Morris Keeton, Clark Kerr, and Howard Bowen (partially) still resort to decentralization in an attempt to surmount the difficulty they see in the hardening lines of emerging interest group politics.[19] Hopefully, with authority vested in a program, department, or institute, rather than in the university as a whole, they reason, the dynamics of small group association will mitigate political divisions and permit faculty, students, and an occasional administrator to work together under consensual arrangements. The university as an organization would become little more than a shield for protecting from the ravages of society the intellectual partnership that exists in the small units. Within academia there is indeed an affinity for Burke's prescription, "To be attached to the subdivision, to love the little platoon we belong to in society, is the first principle (the germ as it were) of public affection."[20]

To get the full flavor of the academician's purpose in opting for a system of governance that protects the autonomy of the small group, it is useful to recapitulate the principal features of the proposal made by the Berkeley Commission on University Governance. Beginning with the premise that procedures suitable for developing intellect should be equally valuable in the intelligent formulation and resolution of political issues, the commission suggested governance by seminars that would lead to something approaching a consensus on institutional policy. To this idea was added the concept of decentralization to allow the autonomous operation of colleges, departments, or programs, depending on which unit constituted a group sufficiently small for all participants to be intimately and vitally involved in the substance and process of teaching and learning. The operating concept would be "intellectually meaningful groups of faculty and students developing curricula and programs as interdisciplinary enterprises." Admission of students, course requirements, resource allocation, and the hiring of nonacademic staff would all be handled at this level.[21]

The academic soul is thus bared in the Berkeley report. Power is dissolved; independent and holistic operations are preserved; decisions are made by a collegium of students and faculty; and quasi-administration is supreme. Governance seminars return to the faculty its role as academic mentor and in so doing preserve faculty exclusivity. Intellectual material becomes the determinant of decisions, and the academician's sense of powerlessness in interest group politics is eliminated. Direct participation without representation is now possible. The Cartesian can cope. Such an approach may be dismissed as impractical, yet it captures the essence of the academic style, not only in the community of the small college but even at Berkeley.

In assessing such a proposal, a trustee, a member of the state legislature, or a state chancellor of higher education immediately sees that it includes no element of accountability for the resources provided by the larger society of which the university is a part. The implication of the Berkeley proposal is that somehow the new faculty-student collegium would operate within the limits of public approbation. Open society's apprehension over removing the constraints of accountability would presumably be relieved by society's faith in loosely defined educational objectives and by the respect it maintains for the professional status of academicians. In desperation, some may conclude that

Robert Wolff was correct when he surmised that academia cannot be governed.

But in the small group arrangement, the academician would probably be the loser. He would be left totally without power, and because power is really about the allocation of resources, which the academician has sometimes assumed to be a birthright, he could indeed find himself in a worrisome position. The public managers would still be free to make drastic shifts in resources among the small groups. If preference were given to the applied programs of business and technology, what would become of the philosopher, pure scientist, or historian?

Other Interpretations

Others have noted some of these same features of the academician's politics, but interpretations vary. In their work on the American college president, Michael D. Cohen and James G. March draw a picture of the academy that is not too different from the view presented here. In institutions of higher education they see ambiguity existing over such matters as the place of political influence and the efficacy of institutional goals. A high level of faculty inertia prevails on matters of change. Information links among the constituencies of a university are weak. Cohen and March also found that before making a decision, academicians are inclined to consider every problem imaginable that might be associated with it. Department and individual status become more important than substance in many decisions, and a concerted effort is made to minimize the role of the administration in the formulation of policy. None of these observations is startling for those who are acquainted with the Cartesian.

In reviewing a number of paradigms that have been used to characterize academic politics, Cohen and March concluded that because universities define their goals so poorly they cannot be characterized by the administrative or bureaucratic prototype of organization. Cohen and March are also uncertain over the applicability of the democratic/pluralistic and the collective bargaining models, principally because of their observation that the separate constituencies of a university do not organize around clear concepts of self-interest. These writers also question whether an elaborate brokerage process functions among constituents of a university. Election results for committee memberships, chairmanships, and other offices do not appear to be linked to what amounts to campaign promises.

All of these concepts, according to Cohen and March, fit poorly with academia. Somewhat timidly, they suggest an anarchial metaphor for academic organization in which neither coordination nor control can legitimately be practiced. In some way, they conclude, decisions emerge from institutional activity without explicit accommodation among constituencies or specific reference to goals.[22] Whatever the misgivings of Cohen and March in making such a suggestion, the politics of the Cartesian amply explain how and why the phenomenon is achieved.

In their work on academicians and the 1972 presidential election, Everett Carll Ladd, Jr., and Seymour Martin Lipset also saw many of these same aspects of academic politics. Their study begins by citing Alexis de Tocqueville's characterization of the intellectual as building an image of an "ideal society in which all is simple, uniform, coherent, equitable, and rational" but which is estranged from the "here and now." They continue by pointing to Richard Hofstadter's view of intellect—the creative side of the mind—which is depicted as the "evaluation of evaluations," or as looking for meaning in a situation as a whole rather than in the sum of its parts. Despite this rationality and an inclination for movement toward an ideal that would seem to assure a progressive outlook, Ladd and Lipset note Clark Kerr's observation that "few institutions are so conservative as universities about their own affairs while their members are so liberal about the affairs of others."[23]

In citing these characteristics, Ladd and Lipset did not attempt to structure an academic paradigm for explaining the politics of a university. Nevertheless, in their work we encounter the political forms of the academician. The view drawn from a composite of Tocqueville, Hofstadter, and Kerr as developed in the Ladd-Lipset study differs in no appreciable respect from the one shaped here using the ideas of Wolff, Oakeshott, and Braybooke and Lindbloom. Certainly, Tocqueville's image will provide a set of relationships that emphasizes rationality and eliminates contention within the university; Hofstadter's characterization reveals the academician's tendency to favor holistic outcomes shaped by "facts" rather than incremental solutions fashioned by "interests"; Kerr's comment rests upon limitations the academician places on progress in order to preserve the academic culture. The allusion to estrangement from the "here and now" translates into the difference in values between the Cartesian house of intellect and the instrumental considerations of our open society.

But Ladd and Lipset question Kerr's view of academia. They point out that the 1969 Carnegie survey found a large majority of professors to be more liberal than conservative, and most professors favored students taking part in university decisions related to course content, admissions policy, and degree requirements. Furthermore, liberalism on such issues was identified with high achievers who are more likely than the plodding members of the academic profession to accept the academic culture attributed in this study to the Cartesian. Is there not a contradiction here? Contrary to the deductions drawn from Tocqueville and expressed by Kerr, the professoriate depicted in the Carnegie survey acknowledged the rights of student interest groups and invited the proponents of pluralistic values to participate in university decision making.[24] They were not so concerned with faculty exclusivity.

The paradox of the Carnegie data when contrasted to Kerr's observation on academic conservatism can be explained if we speculate on some of the assumptions of those responding to the Carnegie survey. Consider again the proposals of Kerr, Bowen, and the Berkeley commission on governance. Each author expressed the prevailing viewpoint among academicians in suggesting a resolution of the university's governance problems by incorporating students into a restructured collegium consisting of a department, college, or institute in which those having a "meaningful role" in academic pursuits would act out small group relationships.

The proponents of this approach see no source of conflict in a solution that invites the practitioners of pluralism into the collegium. The only way to explain their quiescence is to suggest that they have assumed that once the student is introduced into the collegium he will accept the values of the academic culture. To the extent that this assumption is accurate, the results of the Carnegie survey are consistent with the political culture the academician draws from Toqueville's rational and structured world that is divorced from the "here and now" of our contemporary pluralistic society. By assuming that the student can be co-opted and socialized to academic values, the academician has assured that progress will not inhibit his Cartesian sense of individual performance and stability. The ideal of political rationality attributed to the academic culture will be preserved. At the same time, that portion of the academician's consciousness that is associated with our society's egalitarian values will be at peace with itself. An observer cannot but wonder whether upon entering the collegium a student would, in fact, accept the academician's values. Or would he continue to work within his own pluralistic concepts? A certain amount of self-deception might have inadvertently distorted the Carnegie data because the respondents were caught in the contradictions of two separate systems of which they are a part. Moreover, rationality dictates that the mind find a way of accommodating academic and pluralistic values in the same system. Thus the academician is inclined to reach for an explanation that provides an answer to this problem, even though an answer independent of the tensions of pluralism may not exist.

6

Faculty Unions and the Academic Perception

In today's intellectual environment there is a tendency when dealing with specialized institutions (and surely a university fits this category) to ask that writers or theorizers test their suppositions, even when these seem reasonable. The critics want proof. Conclusions based on individual experience are suspect when any effort is made to draw general propositions from them. In concluding this examination of academic politics, a statistical or behavioral summation will not be attempted. Instead, the principles set forth in preceding chapters will be reviewed within the single context of faculty unions. Perhaps such an exercise will demonstrate little more than that the principles are consistent within this single context. But even that degree of validity may help remove any lingering suspicion that the notions presented here could possibly be fanciful.

The advent of faculty collective bargaining provides a useful set of confines within which to review the concepts that have been used to explain the academic endeavor. At the outset let us concede that this device offers only a limited group of institutions for analysis. From the nearly two thousand public and private colleges and universities in the United States that offer bachelors degrees or better, only about three hundred have collective bargaining units representing faculty.[1] At some seventy-five colleges and universities collective bargaining has been rejected. Nevertheless, faculty unionism is contemporary, and it is practiced at a wide variety of institutions in higher education. One view of collective bargaining is that it is antithetical to the academic perception; it represents yet another intrusion of society's values upon the academy. How could it ever be used, a critic might ask, to demonstrate anything about academia and academicians? Certainly, tensions exist between what traditional industrial unions stand for and how academicians have customarily organized their profession. But often it is at a point of tension that behavior becomes explicit. In the presence of tension, we usually do not have to guess about attitudes by considering what is inferred in a situation. People will say what is on their minds. And so it is with faculty unions.

Material for this chapter was drawn from eleven collective bargaining agreements. These were selected almost at random, but they can be placed in categories insofar as they include contracts of faculties in private universities, the state's university, state college systems, and public colleges and universities that have individual rather than systemwide contracts. The contracts also represent a variety of bargaining agents; thus the selection offers a fairly representative sample.

INSTITUTION	COLLECTIVE BARGAIN AGENT
State College and University Systems	
The State Universities of Minnesota	National Education Association (NEA)
New Jersey State Colleges	American Federation of Teachers
Pennsylvania State Colleges and Universities	Independent
The State University	
The University of Connecticut	American Association of University Professors (AAUP)
The University of Maine	NEA
Public Colleges and Universities with Individual Contracts	
University of Cincinnati	AAUP
Western Michigan University	AAUP
University of Northern Iowa	AAUP-NEA
Private Universities	
University of Bridgeport	AAUP
Fairleigh Dickinson University	AAUP
St. John's University	AAUP

Any sample is, of course, open to analysis. Certain things can be said about the conclusions reached from a sample's data simply by observing the distinctions and characteristics of the colleges and universities that are represented in it. A survey conducted by Seymour Martin Lipset and Carll Everett Ladd, Jr., in 1978 suggests some of these distinctions. Unionism has been most acceptable at two-year colleges, which are excluded from consideration in this explanation. Generally it has also seen success at institutions that have experienced the intercession of public sector bureaucratic concepts and where the principal mission is teaching rather than research and scholarship. There appears to be less resistance to collective bargaining among faculty at four-year colleges than at universities having strong graduate components. Individual faculty members who do not join unions, even when their campuses are organized, also appear to be more dedicated to publishing than those who do join the union. Even among bargaining units there are differences. The American Association of University Professors (AAUP) finds much more support at universities than at four-year or two-year colleges. The opposite is true for the National Education Association and the American Federation of Teachers. Members of AAUP also appear to be much more inclined toward publication than those associated with the other two organizations.[2]

These data would seem to suggest that faculty unionism might have an inverse "fit" with the academic political perception of our Cartesian. But this is not necessarily the case. The Lipset-Ladd study found that 75 percent of faculty across the country would vote in favor of collective bargaining even though only 25 percent are actually represented by bargaining agents. Moreover, a review of faculty contracts demonstrates that by and large these do not contradict the academic spirit. Whatever the experience with collective bargaining in industry, when this device falls into the hands of academicians, it is used to serve their purposes—a furtherance of the Cartesian principles.

Thus, we can expect contracts generally to protect the individual by allowing independence in the classroom and freedom of research activities. They will conserve the academicians' most precious commodity—unencumbered time—and they will do what they can to assure the security of a stable environment. We should also expect the drafters of collective bargaining agreements to be preoccupied with the other three Cartesian attributes—rational consideration in all things, objectivity, and no limit on inquiry. Faculty contracts should also demonstrate both the academician's preference for collegiality as a means of organizing his efforts and his suspicion of all authority other than his discipline. The academician's collective bargaining agreements do, in fact, reveal such proclivities.

Although a perusal of their contracts is useful, too much should not be made of faculties' collective bargaining agreements as a guide to how universities operate. In fact, it is not possible to determine procedures and practices at a particular college from a review of the faculty's contract. A great deal of the actual operations of the university is incorporated in custom, informal practice, and governance systems that are not superseded by a contract. Contracts do, however, tell us a great deal about how the academician sees his situation—his relationship to the college or university with which he happens to be affiliated. They are probably most useful for showing what is on an academician's mind. For the purposes of this discussion, therefore, contracts will be used only to gain access to the academician's world.

The Academician's Symbols

A common practice in faculty collective bargaining agreements is to justify the agreement in terms of the mission of higher education and of the university. This is not unusual for a profession that posits its organization on principles rather than goals. The idea of academic mission has already figured prominently in this study. In faculty collective bargaining, an underlying supposition is apparently that the contract will contribute to the college's well-being. Academic freedom is set forth as the principal vehicle by which contract aims will be achieved. Thus, in the New Jersey State College system, "It is the responsibilities of these colleges to provide their students a quality education program, to broaden the horizons of knowledge through research and to make available these resources to the needs of the larger community." The contract continues, "In order to fulfill these obligations, the parties endorse the concepts of academic freedom, professional ethics and responsibilities."[3] Indeed, principles are evoked even to justify collective bargaining.

At other institutions the formula does not vary appreciably.

Pennsylvania

The purpose of the colleges is to create "an intellectual environment which encourages the search for truth." The union and the colleges "recognize that collective bargaining in good faith will further their common aim of offering the best possible educational opportunities."[4]

Bridgeport

The purpose of the agreement is to "insure a healthy and viable institution of higher learning, capable of supporting a qualitative educational program. The agreement aims at maintaining educational excellence, facilitating effective participation in decisions affecting the welfare of the university."[5]

Cincinnati

The intent of the agreement is to "contribute to a healthy and viable institution of higher learning capable of supporting a quality program of teaching, research, and public service. This agreement seeks to maintain educational excellence, facilitate effective faculty and librarian participation."[6]

Western Michigan

Here the parties to the agreement recognize "that a high degree of educational excellence is required to maintain a qualitatively healthy and viable institution of higher learning," and to achieve this end the university and the union "agree to abide by the terms and provisions" of the agreement.[7]

Maine

The board of trustees and the union agree "that academic freedom is essential to the fulfillment of the purpose of the University...[and] to maintain the academic character of the University of Maine as an institution of higher education."[8]

In some agreements, it is not just the contract that is linked to the mission of the college. An active faculty becomes part of the equation. At Fairleigh Dickinson, where the purpose of the agreement is also quality education, the university will achieve its objective by providing for "effective faculty participation in certain decisions affecting the welfare of...[the] University."[9] At St. John's the parties to the agreement simply hope to "improve the quality and effectiveness of education" and to "maintain high standards of academic excellence." But the contract continues, "The faculty is particularly qualified to assist in formulating educational policies and developing educational programs."[10]

Usually, academic freedom is reaffirmed in the language of the 1940 AAUP statement, even at insitutions where AAUP is not the bargaining agent. In a few cases, faculty have managed to extend the sense of the contract beyond freedom and move toward the prized autonomy of our dependent entrepreneur. Thus, at Cincinnati the contract allows faculty a "free search for truth and its free expression" and provides for "full freedom of inquiry, teaching and research not only in the classroom and libraries but in other facets of campus life."[11] The Cincinnati contract does not include the usual admonishment to avoid in the classroom controversial material not an integral part of the course. In the Pennsylvania system, faculty are entitled to full freedom in research, in the classroom, and in the selection of teaching materials. All information related to a member's work is privileged and not subject to disclosure. On campus there is freedom to speak, to be heard, to study, to teach, and to administer. All members of the academic community have freedom of movement and pursuit of their rightful goals.[12]

Faculty contracts state their purpose in an abstract fashion. Any statement that hinges simply upon academic freedom does not reflect the mission of the university in an institutional sense. By and large, contracts are about the individual academician. In this regard, they are the implement of faculty. At the same time, they are not justified from the standpoint of benefits to accrue to faculty themselves. Rather, the benefits are to be enjoyed by a third party—the community in the person of students who are to be afforded academic excellence in teaching as a result of the contract. Thus, the function of the academician under the contract is also his guiding principle. Contracts do not link the interests of the faculty solely to the work of the university. Rather, they tie these interests to its mission, which is then expressed in terms of academic freedom. In this way, contracts affirm the organizing principle of the academician—faculty as university. Contracts are more, therefore, than a recitation of appropriate conditions of work. They are often highly symbolic and actually embody the academician's values. Thus, the attention that they devote to the selfless mission of serving the public should not be surprising.

The essence of an academic career is independence, buttressed by the ascriptive sanction of a terminal degree. This degree more or less certifies the individual academician not simply to teach and engage in research but to teach and study within an academic discipline in some way that allows for a minimum of outside interference. This quality of reserving the position of the individual within an institutional context is found in most faculty collective bargaining agreements. In the New Jersey system, each faculty member is given the right to select the textbooks to be used in his classes, subject only to department procedures. Under this contract no faculty member will be required to teach outside his discipline. The importance faculty associate with the sanctity of the individual's discipline is also seen in the Fairleigh Dickinson contract. The issue in this case is what happens when student enrollments in a discipline are not sufficient to occupy all academicians employed by the department. Before reassigning an academician to teach alien subject matter—even when faculty are facing dismissal because of financial exigency—the administration must attempt to accommodate the individual within his discipline by sharing load, relocating him to another campus, supplementing teaching with nonteaching duties, and sharing an appointment with a nearby college. All these steps are listed in order of preferability, which gives some idea of how the academician feels about his professional world. Only transfer to a totally nonteaching position, part-time status with reduced compensation, or early retirement are considered more noxious than teaching assignments outside the discipline.

This same primacy of the individual is present in the assignment of courses within the discipline. Most contracts suggest that teaching assignments must be negotiated with the individual. Then there is the selection of faculty to teach summer courses, a continuing hassle at most universities. In the New Jersey agreement, the faculty member is given preference over outsiders in staffing summer courses. If an assigned summer course is canceled because of insufficient enrollment, its instructor has priority in other teaching and nonteaching assignments. As in all documents, caveats place limitations on this practice, which, in fact, give administrators discretion. But the general provision sets the tone of the academy. Clearly, consideration for individual faculty is meant to take precedence over institutional concerns. Such an assertion, of course, is unintelligible to the academician insofar as he sees the faculty as the university.

Some contracts go to great length in truly nonenforceable articles to justify the academician's independence. In a much belabored point, the Cincinnati contract asserts with regard to faculty duties and responsibilities, "It cannot be expected that a bargaining unit member perform to a significant degree in all of the aforementioned areas. Accordingly, the responsibilities of individual Bargaining Unit [*sic*] members will vary depending upon the specific areas of activity in which they are mainly engaged."[13] In short, the independence and mix of talents and qualities present in each academician are seen as being unique and virtually sacrosanct. Once again, an effort is made to place the individual above the institution.

There is no reason to doubt the sincerity of what academicians hope to achieve by building a sometimes elaborate superstructure of individuality in their contracts. A contract is not the self-conscious writing of an individual about his profession. It is supposed to be a working document, and whatever the academician hopes to include must have approval of the administrative counterparts at the bargaining table. The drafters are literally writing without a sense of authorship. Contracts are meant to defend and protect the profession. The contract of Western Michigan University makes this point. Among its appendixes is the AAUP Professional Code of Ethics, which states in part:

> His primary responsibility to his subject is to seek and to state the truth as he sees it. To this end he devotes his energies to developing and improving his scholarly competence. He accepts the obligation to exercise critical self-discipline and judgment in using, extending, and transmitting knowledge. He practices intellectual honesty. Although he may follow subsidiary interests, these interests must never seriously hamper or compromise his freedom of inquiry.[14]

This statement is noteworthy insofar as it is the description of an obligation—almost an oath. But this loyalty is to the academician's subject, not his university. Certainly, the Code of Ethics is not simply an allusion to the duties associated with a job, and it is hardly justiciable. The obligation is to grow intellectually without any assurance of ever doing anything other than to teach and to pursue whatever the mind is capable of grasping. Our Cartesian is serious about his creed. There should be little wonder that contracts reflect the unceasing effort to serve the individual.

In reading the AAUP Code, an executive from industry or government might assume that it is little more than a fancy way of talking about professional development. But academicians "develop" in an unusual way. They do not do so as groups, enrolling in special courses or engaging in special on-the-job training. Professional development is a continuing personal process of working alone, going to professional meetings, or perhaps consulting and working in a special nonteaching research institute. Professional development is self-initiated, and faculty contracts devote a great deal of attention to it. Virtually every contract allows for professional travel with some institutional support. There is also the provision for sabbatical leaves—the practice of intellectual renewal by removing oneself from the classroom and perhaps from the college every so often to engage in self-improvement. Two of the contracts (the Minnesota system[15] and Western Michigan) specify that special research funds will be available to support this aspect of academic life. In the case of Minnesota, the union helps establish criteria for distributing funds. At Western Michigan, the faculty research council holds this task, which is the usual practice at universities.

The concern of administrators in these matters is obviously with how far a college or university can go in supporting the individual perception. Their role is to limit the amount of university resources devoted to personal growth. The academician himself could never put a cap on it. In most contracts, the sums available for research are specified, the amounts and the conditions under which faculty can expect support from the university for professional travel are given, and sabbaticals are either limited by a number or proportion of faculty.

Somehow at Fairleigh Dickinson University, administrators permitted themselves to be maneuvered into a costly situation. A quota of sabbatical leaves has been set for each college of the university each year that equals one-seventh of the number of tenured full-time faculty members. In effect, an academic norm has been incorporated into a document that is legally binding on the university. Personal services (principally faculty salaries) can account for 80 –85 percent of a university's costs. With perhaps three-quarters of the faculty tenured, this sabbatical provision alone could consume close to 10 percent of the budget. The university in this case has indeed made a substantial commitment to the development of the individual faculty member. Difficulties and differences over this easement within the Fairleigh Dickinson contract developed as administrators attempted to get the situation under control through the exercise of selective approval of sabbatical leave proposals. A reinterpretation of the contract also helped. The contract, the administration contended, was only meant to allow one-seventh of faculty to apply rather than actually receive sabbatical leave.

Some tension is reflected in the agreements over the locus of decision making on these matters. For the most part, faculty committees award sabbatical leaves with the approval of the president or his designee. The conflict that emerges in deciding how many faculty will

have sabbatical leaves in a year is between the individual pursuits of
the academician and the teaching responsibilities of the university. A
compromise between these demands was achieved at the University of
Maine, where different categories of sabbatical leave are identified as
being granted by the university, campus, division, and department.
Decisions can be made at the corresponding level provided the campus chief administrator approves and no additional costs are incurred.
In effect, a sabbatical leave may be given if peers will assume the
teaching load that would otherwise be carried by the recipient. The
same provision applies at Bridgeport. As a result, an element of self-
regulation by the faculty is introduced into the process of distributing
sabbatical leaves. Less of a sense of institutional control is imposed on
the individual. When peers are prepared to assume a colleague's load,
a sabbatical leave can perhaps be granted.

The compulsion of those who draft collective bargaining agreements
is to enhance the position of the individual while serving the interests
of the university. It can lead to ambivalence in some contracts. On the
matter of sabbatical leaves, the St. John's contract states, "The intent of
this policy is to grant such leaves not to make them difficult to obtain.
Accordingly, the department and the college will make every reasonable effort to accommodate a qualified faculty member's request." But
the contract also cautions, "It is not expected that every faculty member will be granted a leave automatically."[16] The same contradiction on
sabbatical leave reigns in the Pennsylvania system, where the contract
piously intones, "Leaves shall be accumulated so that no one shall lose
entitlement because of failure to use leave."[17] But the contract also
limits leaves to 5 percent of the faculty, a mathematical impossibility if a
leave is allowed for every faculty member after every seven years of
service and leaves that are not taken can be accumulated.

Similar uncertainty prevails at Bridgeport on personnel matters
pertaining to appointment, reappointment, promotion, and tenure of
faculty. Here the president's decisions "shall be based on evidence of
merit in the individual's Personnel File or on institutional need."[18] The
two criteria can, of course, come into conflict. The former requires that
the individual be assessed only on his personal record measured
against what amounts to an abstract standard perceived as "merit"; the
latter permits the comparative judgment that serves the institution but
is abhorred by the academician. In following the rational dictates of the
material in the personnel file, the president is relieved of any possibility
for judgment, but in considering institutional need, personal

judgment by someone other than the academician being assessed can be determinant. Presumably, discretion is left to the president with regard to which guidance he will follow, but he can be sure that his decision will be greeted with loud complaints if it is against the individual. Many administrators, and perhaps even the president at Maine, fail to see the apprehension this discretion can convey to the academician. Almost without thinking about it, the administrator can opt for the decision that reflects "institutional need." At this instant, an action has been taken that looms large for the individual professor. The accommodation that assures his independence has not been made.

In these instances, the implied contradictions in the language of the contracts are obvious. It appears that the academician prefers to behave symbolically by enunciating in his contract the independence of the individual even while accepting an operational situation that almost certainly precludes his achieving individual preeminence. The only alternative to this conflict is to risk seeing the individual perception ignored altogether in the text of the contract—sacrificed to the requirements of the group as determined by someone other than himself. A contradiction in the contract is preferable, even though the academician's craft normally requires that he trade in logical propositions.

The primacy of the individual in academia is reflected by contracts in a variety of other ways. In the Pennsylvania system, information the academician may have about students is privileged, depending on how the professor sees the interests of the student. At Bridgeport, any change in office location is subject to an elaborate procedure insofar as "an alteration of the immediate working environment of a faculty member...may impede the faculty member's work effectiveness."[19] Primacy is afforded the individual at the University of Connecticut by an unusual means. This institution has no effective salary scale or teaching load. Each individual makes his own arrangements with the university. In concept, at least, this is the height of entrepreneurial behavior. Another example of the individual's release from the constraints of a system is evident at Fairleigh Dickinson, where there is no minimum for the time in rank before being eligible for promotion. A guideline exists, and everyone knows the university's practice. But provision is made for cases in which individual qualities are more important than the orderliness that is sometimes supposed to come from uniformity in practice and procedure.

Essentially, all faculty do the same work. Emphasis on teaching as opposed to research will vary from one university to another, but generally the duties are the same. The norms of the profession define them simply as teaching, research, and university-cum-community service. The contracts that were reviewed demonstrate that although this definition prevails, faculty and administrators can be ingenious in how they phrase the formula. One purpose of enumerating duties in contracts is, of course, to allow for personnel evaluation by the university. Conversely, a common thread in contracts is protection of the individual from institutional judgments when evaluation occurs. This can be done in a number of ways. In the Pennsylvania system it is achieved by setting forth responsibilities separate from evaluation criteria. Whereas the former is attached for some reason to the concept of an individual's academic freedom, the latter is associated mainly with institutional procedure. Any effort to structure individual performance according to an administrator's interpretation of institutional requirements can be questioned.

Another ploy is used at Bridgeport, where the contract cites faculty functions without adequately delineating them. Teaching and scholarly or professional achievement are listed as a single criterion for evaluation along with advising students, service, and "additional criteria," in that order of importance.[20] With teaching and research being the most important activities in which an academician engages, evaluation is made more difficult by listing them under the same category. Somehow a single judgment must be made on the two functions. At the University of Maine, the contract carries a special admonition under a section on workload that individual faculty will embody different mixes of functions and responsibilities. Presumably, this determination is left to the individual. In stark contrast with this statement is the listing of responsibilities in ten sometimes overlapping categories that are to be used in evaluation. The sense of the contract seems to violate the details of prescription. At the least, a basis for argument exists if evaluation is attempted on anything other than the norms of the profession.

And here we encounter the preferred means of protecting the individual. It is the practice of stating responsibilities—and presumable criteria for evaluation—as norms that are not enforceable. At Fairleigh Dickinson, under the heading of responsibilities and obligations, a faculty member is called upon to aspire to excellence in teaching, stimulate the intellectual development of his students, strive to keep informed of contemporary developments in his field of specialization, seek to manifest objectivity and fairness in his relations with members of the university community, strive to improve methods of instruction, and recognize diversity. Would any administrator care to deny tenure or promotion because an applicant supposedly did not fulfill one of these obligations? At Cincinnati it is much the same. In this case, the university recognizes "that in the practice of their profession faculty members' principal academic functions are the teaching, discovery, creation, and reporting of knowledge."[21] Could anyone ever be assessed on his discovery of knowledge? As frustrating as these formulations might be to an administrator, for the academician they are delightful manifestations of his independence.

Virtually all definitions of an academician's responsibilities include the idea of service. The term is used loosely. For academia as a whole, it means activity beyond teaching and research or artistic performance that is somehow considered meritorious. Sometimes it is construed narrowly, within the professional competence of the individual being considered. Sometimes it is not. The Western Michigan contract defines community service as "service on state, national, and international boards, commissions, committees, etc."[22] This concept is justified in the contract insofar as the geographic area served by one university is not confined to one locality. In the Cincinnati contract, the definition is narrow—performing committee work in support of the proper and efficient functioning of the university. The same approach is taken at Fairleigh Dickinson, where service is to "the various agencies of governance."[23] Service in this context is apparently unpaid. Some contracts—Western Michigan, Maine, and Minnesota—distinguish outside employment from service. Others clearly include outside employment within the concept of service. Whatever the local practice, virtually all institutions continue fringe benefits during periods of leave without pay when the academician may be working for compensation beyond the confines of the university. The implication here is that the university somehow benefits from this activity. It is service.

All these stipulations may appear to be nothing more than inconsequential personnel business, but they reveal something about the profession that sets it apart. Most important, they emphasize the independent nature of the Cartesian's work insofar as the sections of contracts devoted to service either define or regulate activity undertaken by the individual. Service is not an institutional concept. Outside activity, whether for monetary gain or only for reputation, is actually considered in evaluating an academician's performance for the rewards of tenure and promotion within the university. It thereby becomes a public trust assumed personally by the practitioner. This obligation has very little to do with the university. It is undertaken by the individual because it is the culmination of his profession, not of the particular position he may hold. Only a secondary basis of legitimacy for service is institutional—the mission of the university. As we have seen, in virtually all cases this mission in collective bargaining agreements is phrased as service to the community. Thus, when an academician serves the community, even in ways that are outside his institution (and sometimes his profession), he is seen as furthering the objectives of the college.

It is in such a rationale—always implicit—that an observer can find the roots of much academic behavior. Almost casually, an academician will include church activities and minor political offices in a justification for promotion. A resumé may include an almost endless list of speeches before Kiwanis, the Lions, and other service organizations. Most academicians will say that community service is meritorious in a professional sense because the individual carries the name of the college or university with him. Such activity reflects positively on the institution, and with public approval supposedly will come endowment and increased enrollment. A faculty member who conceals his association with the college while serving in the community will be criticized by his peers and administrators.

When we examine the concept of community service carefully, we see that there is a lot more to it than carrying the name of the college. Deeply embedded in the practices and perceptions associated with the idea of service is the core of the profession. The academician and his institution trade on reputation in a way that is distinct from profit. Esteem is an end in itself, and it is a quality of the individual professor. Only to the extent that the individual garners reputation can it be attributed to his institution. All these relationships are fashioned to display values rather than to achieve an outcome—something that becomes incidental without them. Within this context, the faculty does become the university and the individual does reach ascendancy over the institution. And this awareness is present in the collective bargaining agreements of academicians.

Guarding the Academician's Time

A major point in this book has been the jealousy with which the academician guards his time. A life of teaching and scholarship often involves a conscious decision to give up prospects for high income in exchange for control over one's time. Many academicians are defensive about the lack of public understanding of their profession, particularly the erroneous notion that they work only ten to twelve hours a week— the time they actually spend in the classroom. Faculty collective bargaining agreements reflect a preoccupation with time. In fact, one interpretation of contracts is that the entire organizing motive behind them rests on its protection.

Some contracts include self-serving statements that are apparently meant to explain the academician's point of view on this matter. In dealing with faculty responsibilities, the Cincinnati contract digresses to state that "any one of these functions can of necessity be very time consuming. For example, a teacher normally spends far less time in the classroom than in preparation, conferences, grading papers and examinations, and supervision of remedial or advanced student work."[24] At Maine the apology takes the following form: "University faculty members' service is not measured in a fixed number of hours per week. The faculty member is expected to devote as much time as necessary to fulfill his or her responsibilities."[25] Turning to the Fairleigh Dickinson contract, we find that "teaching load" is set aside for the idea of "academic load, which embraces a much broader range of activities." Moreover, at Fairleigh Dickinson "fulfillment of professional responsibilities cannot be measured by any single time standard."[26]

The touchstone of faculty time is the teaching load required of an academician, combined with other obligations to the university that can be translated into minutes and hours. The limitations that contracts place on load may be expressed as the number of credit hours to be taught in a semester or quarter, the number of separate courses the academician will teach (preparations), hours in the classroom (contact hours), and even the student-faculty ratio or the number of students who can be in a class. Also mentioned are specified office hours, how many students a faculty member must advise, and how all these duties may be grouped in a schedule. Special activities such as theater productions, the coaching of sports, supervision of student teaching, and science laboratory instruction are often quantified by formulas that defy extraacademic understanding.

In most cases co-curricular activities cannot be equated with specific time allotments. Instead, they are listed as an obligation the individual must meet. Surprisingly, three of the contracts that were reviewed made no allusion to workload (Connecticut,[27] Maine, and the University of Northern Iowa[28]). One addressed the matter of overload but not workload (Cincinnati). No conclusion can be reached from these omissions; they reflect local conditions, or "past practice," as contract jargon would put it. But at every university, we may be assured that a clear concept of load exists. The representatives of the faculty at the time the contracts were negotiated at Connecticut, Maine, Northern Iowa, and Cincinnati no doubt concluded that it was not in their interest to enumerate load.

Consideration of the academician's time is reflected in contracts in a variety of ways other than specified workloads. Some contracts state explicitly that teaching during summer session and the carrying of an "overload" will be voluntary, even though this understanding goes without saying at virtually all schools. Among the contracts that make it explicit are those of the New Jersey system, the Pennsylvania system, St. John's, Bridgeport, and Fairleigh Dickinson.

The care that is given to load has ramifications that an outsider often may not fathom. No matter what an academician's load, he is likely to complain about it. Thirty years ago, standard load was five courses a semester. Currently it is four courses at institutions characterized as "four-year teaching colleges" and three or sometimes two courses at research-oriented universities. Whenever a special assignment outside the classroom is suggested by a dean, faculty usually raise the question of "released time," that is, a reduction in teaching load commensurate with the additional responsibilities. Six of the contracts reviewed for this chapter, including those of the three private universities, have provisions for reduced load.

This preoccupation with released time is not just a characteristic of faculty members who are overburdened with research and professional activities. A faculty member whose principal interest is tending his lawn can be equally concerned. Those with reputations as "great teachers" are often singled out for special assignments and may receive a permanent reduced load. Here we are faced with the spectacle of the great teacher who is seldom in the classroom!

This is not to say that faculty are naturally lethargic; far from it. The entrepreneurial sense of the academician usually assures a great deal of "self-starting" activity in any area of university business. The point is that self-allocation of time is a norm of the profession, and faculty pursue this goal almost by instinct—at times without regard for their individual ability to use free time productively in a professional sense.

As a last resort, an academician can always claim that more time can be used simply for contemplation or reflection, and in some cases this assertion has content. As the Maine and Fairleigh Dickinson contracts note, the creation and manipulation of knowledge cannot be timed in a mechanical way. Periods of inactivity are necessary to sort through the implications of thought. Often this task is distinct from writing or preparing for lectures.

Faculty contracts reflect a dual standard on time. The explicit statement is to assure a prescribed limitation on teaching load, office hours, and the like. But many contracts have an ambivalence about "overloads" when these are tied to extra remuneration. Contracts such as those of Western Michigan, St. John's, New Jersey, and Fairleigh Dickinson place a limit on the amount of overload a faculty member can be allotted in exchange for added income. Superficially, it may seem that this limitation would be advocated by administrators who can contend that the quality of instruction will suffer when an individual teaches too much. Some faculty attribute administrators' attitudes on this matter to plain meanness—a desire to limit a resourceful individual's income. But two other factors can also be involved. First is the sense of equity. To the extent that overload, or what industry refers to as "overtime," is considered desirable, all faculty must be given comparable access to it. This notion is certainly not unique to academia.

Another consideration also often comes into play. A pressure within academia over the years has been to reduce the demand that the university can make on the academician's time. Now, in the age of collective bargaining, if a particularly rapacious faculty member seeking paid overload demonstrates that five or even six courses can be taught in a single semester, the academicians' professional argument over the extent to which the university can claim their time is weakened. Perhaps an academician can teach more than three or four courses after all without being overburdened. Thus, sometimes the union itself, representing the collective academic perception, restrains the individual who would otherwise accept "excessive" overload. Someplace within this problem we may encounter the academician's own approach to "featherbedding."

Because an academician will be admonished by peers only under the most severe circumstances, the limitation which faculty unions place on an individual's accepting unpaid voluntary course load is imposed by embodying the spirit of the academic norm—the protection of time—in the legal framework of a collective bargaining agreement. Even then, the union will seldom discipline a member who attempts to exceed the limit. Rather, the administration is held responsible for allowing the contract to be violated by a member of the union!

Our society generally contends that a person cannot rightfully hold two jobs. The assumption behind this view is that one or perhaps both are bound to be neglected and that the employers will not receive their full measure for the compensation they award. In academia this point of view is challenged. The underlying theory seems to be that the classroom is the place where the academician develops knowledge, which he is thereby obligated to take to society beyond the university. Again, values come to the fore, as they always do when social obligation premises action. The result of the academician's obligation to society is the demand that he be free to determine what he will do with his time. It also gives protection against charges of negligence.

An inherent conflict exists between the university, which must extract faculty time in order to assure the group endeavor involved in instruction, and the dependent entrepreneur, who operates in terms of the personal prerogatives he associates with free time. The issue that arises can be one of inattention to duties within a university when an academician is too dedicated to activities outside it. In resolving differences over this matter, most contracts place the burden of proof for negligence on the university. Outside employment cannot be considered contrary to the university's interests unless administrators can demonstrate unsatisfactory performance by that individual within the university. In the contract of the University of Maine, for example, faculty are granted the "right to seek and accept employment beyond their teaching, research and university and public service responsibilities."[29] But, the contract warns, it remains the responsibility of each person to perform fully within the university. Similarly, at Fairleigh Dickinson, each individual may engage in professional consulting provided that such activity "does not interfere with his responsibilities and obligations to the university."[30] The determination is left to the individual. Activity is thereby self-regulated. A common practice in contracts is to require the individual to report outside employment to the university but not to seek permission from the administration to engage in it. There are exceptions. In the Minnesota system, any arrangement outside the university that results in an annual retaining fee or a regular salary requires prior university approval. At Bridgeport, faculty may consult for external organizations one day a week during the academic year. Beyond that, they must have administrative approval for remunerative outside activities.

In most careers, the reasons why duties may have been neglected would never arise in a case of reprimand or dismissal. If negligence becomes apparent on the job, the employer would hardly inquire or even care about its causes. In formulating a position on this issue in academia, contracts also use the approach taken in industry and business, but with a subtle twist. As in industry, the nature of the act of negligence is separated from its cause. But unlike industry, in academia contracts require the university to deal only with the results. Most do not permit it to inquire about cause. In industry, such an inquiry is at the discretion of the employer. It is usually seen as something that will help the employee by perhaps establishing that the source of the difficulty is beyond his control. The underlying premise in academia is not the same. To allow the university to establish causes of negligence, and to view these differently, would soon place limitations on the academician's control of his time. A negative attribute (negligence) could then be tied to something the academician contends is of value to the university and which he insists on doing—engage in outside activity. And he sanctifies the practice by associating values with it, by defining it as a social obligation.

Toward a Stable Environment

A review of faculty contracts by someone not familiar with the academic profession can lead to the conclusion that academia provides a turbulent and uncertain career. When the attention given in contracts to guarding academic freedom is extended with provisions controlling institutional retrenchment for reasons of financial exigency, or termination of programs for the good of the university, and when these are combined with the assiduous care afforded the rights of the individual in any proceedings of dismissal for cause, the reviewer can picture such events occurring daily amid consternation and conflict. Actually, they are unusual. Nevertheless, the bulk of most contracts is devoted to such matters. In this respect, contracts are not about existing conditions. They reflect the apprehension with which the academician watches over not just his independence but also his security. They say something about the torment he experiences by being required to work in an institutional setting.

A statement from the Fairleigh Dickinson contract comes close to saying it all: "The University recognizes that its diverse and multi-faceted faculty represents a major asset, and that security of employment is essential to preserve the atmosphere of intellectual stimulation vital to its academic mission. The University also reaffirms its concern for the lives and careers of its full-time faculty."[31] The individual is of paramount concern in this statement apparently because he is the embodiment of the intellect that defines the university's mission. A major objective of the university is to provide the same tranquillity for this asset that Descartes sought in Holland in order that he might pursue whatever his mind was capable of grasping. In some respects, the academician's quest for security is no different from the assurances sought by individuals in other occupations and careers. Security is a personal objective for virtually all persons having the necessity to earn a livelihood. The academician's purpose, however, extends beyond security. He seeks stability.

Of the contracts that were considered, four (Cincinnati, St. John's, the University of Connecticut, and the New Jersey system) do not include provisions for dismissal of an individual for cause. Presumably, this eventually is covered by university by-laws, past practice, or state civil service regulations. All contracts, however, say a great deal about terminations resulting from retrenchment of programs. In some cases, such as the Minnesota system, the University of Maine, the University of Northern Iowa, and Bridgeport, retrenchment outwardly appears to be an administrative responsibility, although consultation with the bargaining unit is required. The Pennsylvania system requires arbitration on such a decision. At Fairleigh Dickinson, it is turned over to a university commission consisting of faculty, administrators, and students. The union can test any decision of the commission in court before it is implemented. There are lawyers who would question the legality of this possibility. At St. John's University, the perspective of industry and business is reflected insofar as programs may be eliminated and faculty terminated if a program is determined to be seriously deficient by outside evaluation. Using an analogy from industry, we could rephrase the St. John's provision to say that if the product is shoddy and the company cannot compete in that line of goods, then the section within the plant that produces this item will be closed down.

The proposal most antithetical to the academic perception of stability was probably found at Western Michigan University, where a student-faculty ratio of less than 17.5 to 1 permitted the "laying off" of faculty. In turn, the university was bound to rehire these people when the ratio passed 18.5 to 1 and to increase faculty when it exceeded 19.5 to 1. Under such conditions, there could be no stability. It would indeed be unusual if in actual practice this article were even applied. And, in fact, it never was. The union and the university could not even agree on a definition for a full-time equivalent faculty member from which to calculate the ratio. In the subsequent contract the provision was deleted. This approach tended to quantify the faculty's function—to deal with teachers as indistinguishable units within a group. To the contrary, the academician sees his work in individual and qualitative terms. The idea of adjusting faculty size to stabilize a student-faculty ratio could only be repugnant to the academician.

Whatever authority a contract may vest in the administrators of a college and the board of trustees to initiate retrenchment, the mere requirement of consultation with the faculty or its bargaining unit before proceeding conceals a laborious procedure of review—consideration of every possible alternative to the actual firing of faculty members. One can imagine a process that would exhaust even the most efficiency-minded administrator. The full implications of what would happen at most universities under these circumstances is explicit in the contract of the University of Cincinnati.

At Cincinnati, before terminating tenured faculty, or untenured faculty during their term of appointment, the administration must provide the faculty union with the information that would support any declaration of financial exigency. This information must include the savings that the administration believes necessary to overcome the financial difficulties of the institution. In fact, all of the university's finances would become the topic of discussion. On the basis of either separate analysis or a joint statement from the union and the administration, the board of trustees at an open meeting can then declare a state of financial exigency. A joint financial exigency committee having faculty representation equal to that of the administration is then formed to develop a plan to meet the crisis.

This committee would operate under four constrictions in making its recommendations: (1) Funds generated by one college could not be transferred to another. (2) Before retrenchment of faculty, budgets would be cut and activities eliminated for programs that are (a) not self-supporting, (b) not in direct support of academic programs, or (c) not essential for the continuation of the general academic program. (3) Due consideration must be given to providing students with a means of completing the requirements of an affected program. (4) Affected faculty must be informed and the financial exigency committee will consider alternatives proposed by faculty from the affected academic units for effecting equivalent budget reductions. In addition, the committee could investigate all existing unrestricted funds and make recommendations on how these could be used to overcome the emergency. It is of incidental interest that the programs mentioned in item 2 are apparently those in which no faculty are involved. Presumably other employees of the university could be terminated. So much for union solidarity.

Any proposal having support from five members of the fourteen-member committee would be presented to the board of trustees. Students and faculty not on the committee could also present their views to the board. The entire process would require a minimum of 150 days, and faculty who were to be terminated would receive up to a year's salary in addition to payments for the remainder of the operating year.

In a similar but separate process, the administration at Cincinnati can under the contract determine that the long-range educational mission of the university as a whole necessitates the termination of a program, department, or college even though this action will result in the discharge of faculty. In this case, "the reasons which the Board shall consider shall be based entirely on the consideration that the long-range educational mission of the college is enhanced by the discontinuation. These reasons shall not include cyclical or temporary variations in enrollment, nor shall they be primarily based on possible financial advantages which might accrue should the discontinuation occur."[32]

The citing of these provisions does not necessarily give us a blueprint of what might happen at Cincinnati if an exigency were proposed or the deletion of a program were recommended. The stipulations do make it doubtful, however, that the termination of a faculty member could ever occur under them. Neither stipulation, in fact, has ever been invoked. Faculty were, of course, discharged from the Wisconsin system beginning in 1974/75. But the route of the financial exigency in a public system is indeed difficult. The exigency may be declared, but in most cases this action would have the political purpose of putting the state legislature under pressure to provide more funds. Because allocations in most states are annual, the requirement at Cincinnati to pay many faculty for the operation year and one subsequent year defeats the purpose of discharging faculty to save money. Then there is the matter of honoring the public trust—assuring that all students in affected programs at Cincinnati have an opportunity to complete their courses of study.

The discontinuation of programs at Cincinnati under conditions other than a financial crisis would be close to impossible. With the academician's notions of program integrity and given his tendency to see the benefits of program development without consideration for costs, how could faculty ever be convinced that discontinuing a program actually enhanced the mission of the university as a whole, particularly when financial advantage and temporary variations in enrollment cannot be considered? How, in fact, can variations in enrollment be determined a permanent rather than a cyclical or temporary phenomenon? Programs at Cincinnati have been terminated, but not under this provision of the contract. What we actually see at Cincinnati, to the extent that the contract can be interpreted by faculty, is the prescription for a stable environment.

Collegiality

All faculty contracts focus on the accommodation between institutional authority and the faculty. When faculty can achieve what they wish from a contract, considerations of the collegial department will stand out in this relationship. As we have seen, collegiality is the academician's preferred method of organizing his efforts when called upon to work in a group. One of the most comprehensive statements reflecting the faculty viewpoint is to be found in the Western Michigan document.

> By virtue of their command of their discipline, University faculty have as a unique resource the abilities to assist in the governance of departments in which they exercise their respective disciplines. Faculty, therefore, should participate in the governance of their departments in order to create and maintain harmonious relationships among colleagues, and to fashion and maintain the departments in such a way as to make them maximally appropriate for instruction, research, service and other professional activities of the discipline. Fundamentally, what is desirable and what is intended by the sections that follow is to insure meaningful participation by departmental faculties, with the ultimate power of decision-making by Western, but with an assurance of procedural regularity and fair play.[33]

In this statement we confront the academician's view of suitable institutional practice. Personal identity is to be found in academic discipline, not in the university. Discipline is the means by which the academic mission—instruction, research, service, and other professional activities—is to be achieved. Direction within the department is provided by emphasizing harmony among those who share the discipline. With this prescription, the academician achieves the cherished stability. But for harmony to prevail in our utopian community, there must be limitations on outside interference. As the Western Michigan contract stated, institutional authority is limited by the necessity for "procedural regularity and fair play," the antithesis of decisions that are capricious and arbitrary. In effect, it means that direction for the conduct of the university's business will come from the affirmation of academia's norms. Insofar as faculty contracts reflect the academic political culture, they can be expected to include these attributes.

In protecting his identity, the academician's first step is to assure integrity within the discipline. In the Bridgeport contract, therefore, the department determines the appropriate terminal degree for its members and recommends for the dean's approval an appropriate equivalent for this degree when candidates for appointment or promotion would otherwise not qualify but have outstanding professional experience. This departmental authority is exercised with limitations, however, for "if the dean wishes to apply a higher standard, the department shall ordinarily be expected to concur."[34] In the New Jersey system, the department also determines the equivalent of the terminal degree. Because the terminal degree constitutes the ascriptive quality within the academic identity, there is a certain logic in allowing only those who hold this identity to determine any substitute for it. But in the stipulation of the Bridgeport contract that permits the dean to set a higher standard, we see the first interplay between the academician with his discipline and the university with an authority that goes beyond it.

Another practice that relates to collegial protection of disciplinary identity is cited in the contracts of Fairleigh Dickinson and the Pennsylvania system, where a department representative periodically observes the classroom sessions of both tenured and nontenured faculty members. This routine can be controversial insofar as it is seen as treading upon the independence of the individual academician. Usually, such features of collegiality are not formally established. But if a faculty member is physically or mentally incapacitated and insists upon performing teaching duties anyway, a department will often be stirred to action and observe classroom performances as a step toward removing a colleague from his position. The implication of such a move is that in the final analysis, the integrity of the discipline must be protected, even at the expense of the individual, and this can be done only by the collegial group. At times a department is hustled into this position when a dean becomes aware of a problem in instruction and insists on entering the classroom himself. Suddenly, disciplinary integrity takes on a new dimension, and the department insists on assuming the responsibility of classroom observation for itself.

An approach to group identity present at Western Michigan allows the department to maintain the official personnel files of faculty. Dispersed official files can become an administrative nightmare. Uniformity cannot be assured, and without uniformity, all sorts of charges by grievants over irregularities can be lodged against the university, even though it may not have a way of establishing control over files held by thirty or more subunits. Yet, the academicians' thinking on this matter is not difficult to understand. In a symbolic way, the department's maintaining files also makes it the guardian of the academicians' identity.

Under contracts, departments usually retain the right to organize themselves. This privilege, too, is inherent in the meaning of collegiality. But in today's organizationally conscious world, a minimal structure is required by the university. Thus departments do not have exclusive initiative in fashioning their structure. The advent of faculty unions has added a further element of uniformity to organization by requiring some sort of department personnel committee. As in the Pennsylvania system, this committee will often determine its own rules, and when they vary too much from department to department, trouble is afoot. Contracts generally allow faculty members more leeway in grieving on procedural errors than on matters of substance. Academicians relish the opportunity to make distinctions, and when procedures for reviewing the applications of all candidates for promotion are not uniform (even when it is due to departmental variance), objections will surely surface. Thus, collegial practice can be detrimental to the administrative interests of the total university.

Beyond preserving academic identity and rights of organization, most contracts deal in some way with departmental authority. At Western Michigan University, the group's prerogatives are carefully delineated to include not only rights of organization—to establish committee structure, select committee members, and set the terms of departmental officers (except chairmen)—but they also include the privilege of establishing a department's criteria, policies and procedures for tenure, promotion, appointments, sabbatical leaves, and merit promotions. Degree requirements for students, curricular offerings, budget guidelines, teaching assignments and class scheduling, and the definition of workload are all responsibilities of the departments at Western Michigan. Most actions are limited by the necessity to be in accordance with university policy. Similarly, at Bridgeport, departments determine curriculum, allocations within their budget allotments, requirements for students majoring in their discipline, and the status of individual faculty members.

Perhaps the most collegial approach to organization of the contracts reviewed is at Fairleigh Dickinson University, where a department policy committee appears to share with the chairman the day-to-day direction of the department. The result could be group management, the essence of collegiality. An individual faculty member would seldom transact business with the dean under a strict application of the terms of this contract. In the case of reduced load, for example, the individual does not apply; the department recommends—at least that is how the contract reads.

To an outsider it would appear that too much authority vested in departmental committees would be contrary to the independence sought by the individual academician. But with the automatic manner by which work is distributed as a result of prescriptively assigned duties, direction by the department becomes secondary. Then, too, all members of the committee directorate at Fairleigh Dickinson are academicians themselves. Such a committee, therefore, will, in all probability, function to assure that protection is afforded the individual. It is much more difficult for a dean to discipline an academician if the dean must operate through a departmental committee. Without the committee, confrontations are between two individuals under conditions in which one (invariably the faculty member) feels that he has little authority. At Fairleigh Dickinson, the dean, speaking in the name of the university, must confront the department. Somehow the contest seems more even.

But fear of punishment or interference is not all that rankles the academician. Administrators are usually identified with judgments by which one academician is selected for special privilege over another. Interpersonal comparison stands out in these decisions. Recognition for a colleague, of course, is not always viewed negatively by a department. Nevertheless, most academicians prefer that any such distinction for a member of the group first have the approval of peers. Contracts provide for this practice. It is the essence of collegiality.

Although academicians organize themselves into departments, a repeated theme of this book has been that essentially they work alone. Because of this practice, it has been noted that usually academicians do not vest their organization with a great deal of authority over the individual. They prefer that the institution's operations be self-regulating with behavior determined by norms rather than rules. In faculty collective bargaining agreements, therefore, much of the authority exercised by departments is not expressed as specified actions that the group will take. Rather, contracts allow departments the privilege of setting criteria for action to be taken by the individual. Departmental direction, therefore, is generally expressed in passive ways. In fact, authority is even less direct. Often the criteria are not for what the individual will do. Instead they are for the evaluation of what he does by departmental peers. As a result, it sometimes appears that the academician does not even operate under the direction of the collegial group. He works independently in ways that will elicit its approval. Within this context, the portion of contracts concerned with the department usually centers attention on membership and status (rank) within the group. On matters pertaining to departmental operations, contracts contain provisions that ward off administrators, confirm accepted practices, and evaluate how closely a member of the department observes norms. Departmental administration can become almost nonexistent.

A few examples of the "criteria syndrome" can be seen in the contracts of the New Jersey system, Cincinnati, and Western Michigan, where departmental committees establish the criteria for promotion and tenure. In each case, the decisions embodying these criteria must have the approval of or be reached in cooperation with the university's administration. But, in turn, the action of the administration is often prescribed. At St. John's, the contract includes the admonition that on questions of curriculum, research, and faculty status, when the administration exercises the "power of review," its decisions "shall ordinarily concur with faculty determinations."[35] A similar sense is found at Cincinnati, where the contract requires substantial reason for an administrator to differ with departmental recommendations. Such a relationship lends itself poorly to regulation.

Maine, Northern Iowa, the University of Connecticut, Fairleigh Dickinson, Bridgeport, and Western Michigan all provide for departmental initiative in faculty evaluation. In most cases, evaluation is specified in contracts for faculty members who have not yet received tenure or who are seeking either promotion or some distinction through meritorious recognition. Otherwise, the professoriate proceeds without a formal assessment, even by peers. When evaluation does occur, initial assessment is usually by a department committee limited to tenured faculty. Of the six contracts cited above, only that of the University of Connecticut does not include a provision for student evaluation. Most contracts appear to reflect a certain discomfort with this practice. At Maine, student evaluation is justified as a means of improving instruction, while at Western Michigan it is defined but apparently not mandatory. In all cases, the instrument of evaluation, if specified at all, is developed and the evaluation itself is conducted by the department. At Northern Iowa the administration is given the somewhat threatening prerogative of determining a standard component of the evaluation questionnaire after consultation with the student association and faculty union.

Most contracts devote considerable attention to appointments. Membership, of course, stands at the center of collegiality. The contracts that are most restrictive in terminology, if not in practice, are at Maine and in the Pennsylvania system, where the president may reject any new appointment. The Maine contract specifies somewhat redundantly that this decision is not subject to a grievance. At Bridgeport, a truly cooperative atmosphere is foreseen, in which "the department and its chairperson, together with the dean, shall make new appointment recommendations to the VPAA"[36] (vice-president for academic affairs). In New Jersey, "the Colleges...recognize the value of peer consultation and except in unusual circumstances will consult with the involved department concerning the procedures to be used in any particular case for appointment and reappointment."[37] The contract of the Minnesota system, which seems to reflect a situation in which the administration has held a great deal of authority, simply states that the president shall involve departments in evaluating credentials and in making recommendations for new appointments.

The St. John's contract allows the administration unusual authority and in some respects violates collegiality insofar as initiative does not always rest with the department in faculty appointments. Appointments can be made when "the Administration deems it appropriate to infuse new life into a department." In this instance, "to solve problems of obsolescence," the president may request a department to search for a faculty member having specific qualifications. Ultimately, the president may make an appointment without the recommendation of the department.[38]

A novel treatment of collegiality on questions of appointments is practiced at Cincinnati. In this case, when the dean and the department disagree on a new appointment, the academic vice-president will, through a complex process that allows for an ultimate faculty voice, appoint a committee of five faculty members to resolve the difference. It will include members from the department, from the same discipline outside the department, and from related disciplines. The university, therefore, in the person of administrators, does not overrule a department. But because most of those on this committee will be faculty members from outside the department concerned, the concept of departmental collegiality is obscured. The outside member, having a strong sense of the university or some uneasiness over future relations with the dean, may decide against a department. Conversely, when placed in such a position (as when faculty function as a collegewide promotion and tenure committee), the outsider may be guided by the department's preference. At best, it is not a comfortable position for the extradepartmental member. The saving grace of the situation is that this contract provision has never been used.

But again we must look to the Fairleigh Dickinson contract for the complete academic perception. On the matter of new appointments, it specifies that "the College Dean shall normally concur with the recommendation of the department except for substantial reasons which shall be stated in writing."[39] In addition, the College Faculty Status Committee, consisting of seven faculty members and two students, can give advice to achieve agreement when department and dean are unable to settle on an appointment. If accord still eludes the department and the dean, the entire search and appointment procedure will be repeated! And so the merry-go-round proceeds until an understanding is reached. Sanity may be sacrificed in such a procedure, but collegiality and departmental prerogatives are preserved. The reader is again reminded that procedures stipulated in faculty contracts reflect only in an approximate manner what might actually transpire at a particular university. At Fairleigh Dickinson in fact, the procedure was changed to give the vice-president something approaching the powers of cloture and resolution in debates between deans and departments.

Few contracts resolve the matter of the collegial department's role in the overall business of the university. Generally, when contracts move beyond the status of members and criteria for their professional behavior, there are platitudes. The mood is reflected by the Maine contract, which states, "The departments, divisions, or other appropriate units shall retain their traditional input into academic policy and standards....They shall establish appropriate committees to carry out their responsibilities pursuant to this agreement."[40] In what amounts to an unenforceable dictum, the Bridgeport contract states that "institutional needs" will be determined by the department and the college.[41] At Fairleigh Dickinson, the contract holds that "primary...academic responsibilities are in a department."[42]

The Bridge to University Authority

The chairmanship of a department is the nexus of collegiality and institutional authority. The strains inherent in the position often are not apparent from observing the operations of a college. Nor in the past have some chairmen been able to identify some of the less comfortable aspects of their situation. Collective bargaining, and the attending necessity for specifying the roles of actors on the university scene, have brought a growing conclusion that in many instances the chairman, as neither fish nor fowl, occupies a difficult position.

The very citing of the role of the chairman highlights the uneasy feelings of administration and faculty alike over the office. Each can easily conclude that someone from the "other side" is being trusted with its business. The St. John's contract, a relatively limited document that relies heavily on past practice, goes to some length to explain the position: "The Department Chairman is at the same time a faculty member with respect to his teaching obligations as well as serving as the departmental liaison to the Administration. As the academic leader of his department he is obligated to represent its interests and serve its welfare. In an equal sense, the Departmental Chairman has the professional responsibility to consider the departmental needs in conjunction with the overall interests of the University community."[43] The contract of the University of Maine follows much the same formulation with the statement that "chairpersons have both administrative and collegial functions and...[department] members have a legitimate concern in the selection, retention and performance of individuals serving as chairpersons."[44]

At most universities, contracts specify that the appointment of the chairman is a joint responsibility. Usually, as at Bridgeport, within the New Jersey system, and at St. John's University, the department initiates the selection and the administration confirms. At St. John's, the contract also states that appointments of chairmen should normally be in conformity with department members' judgment. At Bridgeport and also at Fairleigh Dickinson, the dean is expected to approve the nomination if it has the support of two-thirds of the department's members. In this stipulation, we find the added weight given to a decision by the academicians' affinity for consensus. Certainly, in the face of a consensus, the administration is less likely to assert itself. On the other hand, mischievious deans are often tempted to play when a department appears to be of two or three minds about the appropriate nominee for chairman.

In some cases, the language of contracts reflects greater initiative for the administration in the selection process. At Cincinnati, the administration nominates the chairman after consultation with a departmental committee. The same perception applies in the Pennsylvania system, except the department may then reject the nominee. In either case, the actual practice is difficult to determine from the contract. There may, in fact, be considerable departmental discretion in either of these situations. The president's role in appointing a chairman at the University of Maine appears to be much more definite than at other universities in that he "may accept or reject the recommendation of the department and that decision shall be final."[45] The president may also fill the position on a temporary basis (presumably without a departmental recommendation) for a maximum of one year.

Some schools, notably specified campuses of the University of Maine as well as Fairleigh Dickinson and Western Michigan, preclude the chairman from belonging to the faculty union. This stipulation, in effect, is meant to set the chairman apart from faculty and to emphasize the administrative nature of his position. Other contracts, such as those of the University of Connecticut and Maine, call attention to the possibility of appointing a new member to the faculty specifically for the purpose of becoming chairman. This approach may be expected to result in a chairman who is not too cozy with faculty in conducting his administrative responsibilities.

A common and somewhat surprising practice in view of most chairmen's origins on the faculty is for a department to eliminate from the collegium the individual who occupies the chair. This is achieved by excluding him from membership, or at least voting membership, on the committees that evaluate peers or act on reappointment, promotion, or tenure. This practice is followed at Cincinnati, Bridgeport, and in the Pennsylvania system. Usually the chairman has a voice on all such matters, but it is a distinct voice—a judgment rendered separate from the collective wisdom of the department. In some cases, this separation of decision-making responsibilities is structured to limit the authority of the chairman. In others, competing forces appear to be at work. Thus, in the Minnesota system, the chairman seems to hold the balance of authority insofar as departmental committees are only supposed to assist him. But in the same contract, a somewhat different impression is given by the expectation that the chairman will reflect "the majority faculty sentiment."[46] Much like the situation at Fairleigh Dickinson, the Minnesota contract suggests that chairmen may have authority but that departmental committees serve as a shadow government that tracks their actions and is empowered to submit to deans and vice-presidents a collective judgment that stands side by side with the chairman's own. But again, it is difficult to determine how a university actually operates from the reading of a contract. Faculty perceptions, however, are explicit in most agreements. To the extent that the chairman represents the administration, he must be viewed distinct from the collegium and its purposes, even though personally he may be a faculty colleague of long standing.

The authority of the chairman per se is limited by collegiality, whatever his administrative attributes. Much as for the department as a whole, his authority is phrased in terms of the opportunity to comment upon the performance of peers rather than to tell them what to do. His influence is in his independent recommendations on appointment, tenure, promotion, and possibly sabbatical leaves. Curriculum remains firmly in the hands of the group, where individual initiative and even license are tolerated on course selection and often in scheduling. But the chairman's word has weight because of his access to the administrative echelon of the university—often more weight than is afforded faculty committees. A chairman, therefore, who necessarily trades on the authority of the administration, can become intimidating to peers.

The framework of departmental decisions reveals a wide variety of perceptions with regard to what is taking place when a chairman does act. At the one extreme is the Western Michigan contract in which all authority within the university is enumerated under two headings—

"administrative" and "faculty."[47] The decisions of chairmen are listed with the former. This is consistent with the exclusion of chairmen from the bargaining unit and a specific prohibition at Western Michigan against faculty considering the selection of chairmen a departmental prerogative. At the other extreme are our collegial friends at Fairleigh Dickinson. Here the chairman proceeds with the reminder that he is "a facilitator and implementor of departmental policies and spokesman for the department within the University and the larger community. He speaks in the name of the department in responding to inquiries."[48] This is not exactly an explanation that verifies an authoritative position for chairmen. At St. John's, the chairman appears to be an integral part of the department's group process and is expected to operate comfortably without independent judgment. Essentially he is the initiator of departmental business who functions jointly with committees of his peers and colleagues. He is the first among equals.

The final factor that shows the uncertainty with which departments view their own chairmen is expressed in the agreements of St. John's, Bridgeport, and the Minnesota system. In these cases, the departments may initiate recall proceedings. At St. John's, only 30 percent of the faculty need request such an action, and a chairman is removed by a majority vote of the department.

University Authority

The distinction academicians make in separating a chairman from the collegium only provides the first glimpse of how they treat authority with its institutional features. Once we center our attention on the university itself, collective bargaining agreements truly reveal the suspicion with which administration is held and the uncertainty of faculty over administrators' intent.

Contracts are constructed to assure the prerogatives of both academicians and administrators. But the authority claimed by each is not necessarily stated. Usually it is implicit, being defined by what is not rather than what is said in the contract. Agreements have very little to say, for example, about budgets and the financial matters of the university. Yet, we assume these are the responsibilities of the administration. In a somewhat less conclusive manner, contracts say little about academic programs. These, we assume, belong to the faculty.

But faculty authority is not exclusive. Budgetary decisions and those who make them will eventually impinge upon the academic program.

The lengthy article on the procedure for discontinuation of an academic program found in the contract of the University of Cincinnati points to an administrative transgression across the imaginary line we have just drawn between academic program and institutional finances. Recommending the discontinuation of a program at Cincinnati falls to the administration with the decision being taken by the board of trustees. The best faculty can do to protect themselves in this situation is to require that the arguments used in the recommendation and the reasons for which the act is taken "shall be based entirely on the consideration that the long range educational mission of the University as a whole will be enhanced by the discontinuation."[49]

The weakness of the academician is all too apparent. To give itself some protection, the faculty at Cincinnati has literally invited the administration into an area it would otherwise reserve for itself. Administrators are no longer confined to financial considerations. They are now dealing with the educational mission of the university, and they are making a qualitative judgment about it. But at least by accepting this degree of administrative intercession, the faculty will assure that the decision on discontinuation of program will be defined in ways that the academician can understand rather than through the alchemy of institutional finance. In the process, faculty will be able to argue more effectively against any proposed discontinuation.

Although most of the contracts that were reviewed do not discuss discontinuation of programs as such, they do deal with the matter obliquely in their treatment of retrenchment. And the preferred faculty vehicle in most contracts is to limit retrenchment to discharge of faculty by seniority within programs. Ultimately, the administration makes the decision as to which program is to be affected. Within limits, this decision can be selective with regard to the department that is singled out for special attention. In the final analysis, not even the ascriptive pretensions of an academician toward his discipline are protected. Someone who does not share in it will in all probability make the decision on program reduction or elimination.

Even the symbolism associated with such acts seems to work against the academician. Any retrenchment is a confrontation between the limitations inherent in the administrator's culture of resources and the expansiveness of the Cartesian's ever-growing intellectual universe. And in this contest the administration has the advantage of assuming the identity of the college. Thus, in discussing retrenchment, the contract of the Pennsylvania system allows the administration to become the "Commonwealth/Colleges."[50] In the New Jersey system, the president suddenly becomes the "college" when drawing the distinction between his role and that of the faculty on matters of appointment.[51] The only institutional identity from which the faculty can draw authority is "the department," hardly a designator reflecting the same power as that claimed by the president. The language of the contract at Western Michigan University clearly shows the real meaning of this lack of equality in institutional symbols between faculty and administrators. In discussing departmental governance, the contract ensures "meaningful participation by departmental faculties, with the ultimate power of decision-making by Western."[52] And who is "Western"? We can only assume it to be the administration operating under authority granted by the board of trustees. This imagery is diametrically opposed to the preferred symbol of the academician—faculty as university. It does, however, confirm a point that was made earlier, namely, that in the public's eye the administration holds the identity of the university.

In this regard, contracts have been damaging to faculty insofar as they serve to confirm the administrator's claims. Union contracts are an occasion for all things appearing to be done in the name of the president. Agreements are replete with the phrase "the president or his designee." The administration of a college thereby assumes the characteristics of a monolith. Administrative authority is emphasized. In the days before collective bargaining, this was seldom the case. Even today, this concept does not reflect the loose, nondirective nature of most academic administration when the justiciability of a contract is not the point at issue. Whatever the intent of faculty in organizing for purposes of collective bargaining, they have pushed administrators toward an even greater bureaucratic perception than they might already have held. Unless the contract is unusual, administrators eventually attempt to assume greater responsibility because of it. Somewhere in the process they go beyond the idea of exercising authority with faculty tolerance—a condition that upholds faculty imagery. Collective bargaining has made more things explicit, and faculty can no longer claim that they hold a benign but real rein on institutional power.

To assure stable and smooth operation of the university, academicians and administrators do work together, even under union contracts. Most contracts condone a practice by which faculty initiate action on matters that concern them and administrators confirm. In these instances, practice does permit the faculty to act out the exercise of benign authority. Matters on which the individual perception of the academician intersect with the institutional outlook of the administrator are, again, those related to educational policy and personal status—curriculum, graduation requirements, and regulations on grading in the one category and personnel evaluations, appointments, promotion, tenure, and professional leave in the other. In these areas, authority is said to be shared—the faculty, usually in the form of departments and collegewide committees, is permitted to make recommendations.

The procedure used at most universities is one of consultation, and decisions are expected to show some evidence of the exchange of views that takes place. In this process, the niceties or civility of the faculty-administrator relationship are observed. The administration must meet with the faculty and "give reasons" for rejecting faculty recommendations on personnel actions. In the process of establishing criteria for peer evaluation at Maine, if the chief administrative officer rejects the proposal of a department, a panel of three faculty and three administrators will resolve the issue. The panel's findings are binding on both parties. In the Jersey system, a president who rejects a chairperson elected by a department must also give reasons either in writing or "informally in person to a department at a meeting called for the purpose."[53] At Fairleigh Dickinson, reasons are automatically required of a dean who differs with a department over the selection of a chairman or the appointment of a new faculty member.

In the Minnesota system, the requirement applies to the appointment of chairmen; in Pennsylvania, reasons must be given for the president's rejection of a new appointment proposed by a department. The same applies when the president refuses to renew the contract of a faculty member or disapproves a department's recommendation for appropriate equivalencies for the terminal degree. At Western Michigan, reasons are required when a chairman, dean, or vice-president does not approve committee structure, criteria for tenure and promotion, or procedures for recommending tenure and promotion, sabbatical leaves, degree requirements, curriculum revisions, budget allocations, teaching assignments, schedules, or definitions of workload. Invariably, every reason (actually a judgment under these circumstances) inspires a counter, and the business of the university can quickly be reduced to the deliberations of a debating society.

On the denial of tenure or termination of services, the Western

Michigan contract includes a curious provision, possibly inserted at the insistence of the administration almost as a threat against faculty.

> It may not always be to the advantage of the faculty member to be informed of the reasons, particularly in writing. If he/she is informed of them, he/she can be placed under an obligation to divulge them to the appointing body of another institution if it inquires why he/she is leaving his/her present position. Similarly, a written record is likely to become the basis for continuing responses by Western to prospective appointing bodies and may jeopardize his/her chances for obtaining positions over an extended period.[54]

Despite what appears to be a rather heavy-handed rejoinder by the administration at Western Michigan, total administrative discretion in approving or disapproving faculty recommendations is not accepted as a matter of course. In fact, there is often a substantial constraint on administrative action. "Giving reason," from the standpoint of an academician is an essential bit of business. It is not simply a procedure by which an administrator justifies a decision. It is shaped to reinforce the relationship between administration and faculty, neither of which is expected simply to go its own way. Whatever the merits of any particular case, the language of contracts often implies that consideration should be given by those making the decision to the faculty's point of view. In some cases, of course, this is only a ceremonial and symbolic act of expressing regard for faculty prerogatives. But even then, it is surprising how often the mere acknowledgment of their position will satisfy faculty.

Another practice that no doubt reveals the academician's discomfort in the presence of institutional authority is the insistence of faculty on some campuses that union representation be introduced into the governance system. Governance, of course, preceded all unions and has been established almost as custom at older universities. Years ago it was codified in the rules and regulations of many colleges. What amounts to a charter can be found in faculty handbooks or the body of documentation developed by a faculty senate, which in its own right may hold the mandate for establishing university committees and maintaining departmental practice.

Why, then, blend governance with unions? One answer may be that once collective bargaining is accepted, a distinction can no longer be made in academicians' minds between bargaining unit and faculty because of the holistic nature of the academic process. The emphasis the academician places on the style by which things are done within the Cartesian prescription precludes any artifical separation of the conditions from the content of work. Everything must fit together rationally. Thus it must be considered as one. But in addition, the link between union and governance gives the academician assurance. For faculty, the union is a countervailing expression of authority that balances whatever power they see in the hands of the administration. Hopefully, the union may allow the academician a greater voice in the operation of the university, or perhaps simply assure his independence for professional pursuits.

In some cases, such as Fairleigh Dickinson University, faculty do not actually introduce the bargaining unit into governance. But they do cite the structure and authority of the governance system in their contracts. Whatever discretion custom might have allowed faculty in the conduct of the business of the university, the administration must now confirm this practice by signing on the dotted line in a legally binding contract. In these instances, however, the beneficiary from the contract is not exactly the "bargaining unit." It is the faculty insofar as governance is a concern of this broader institutional concept. The conflict between these two identities, once a faculty organizes itself as a collective bargaining unit, is implicit in the judicial decision of the suit by Yeshiva University to prevent its faculty from organizing. In this case, a judge held that the faculty could not organize because through governance they participated in the management of the affairs of the institution.[55] Collegiality is dedicated to this purpose.

The notion of working within a dual concept of identity was reviewed in Chapter 4. Despite some faculties' uncertainty about it, the idea is worthwhile because difficulties arise when the identities become intermingled. As a union member, an academician does not operate in an independent, holistic, and ascriptive fashion. He is meant to be "organized." That is the purpose of a union. With a blurring of the academic identity, primacy is sometimes not given to the mission of our academic practitioner. Attention turns to matters other than devoting one's life to the development of individual reason.

The academician has, of course, adapted collective bargaining to his style of performance, but little by little unionism leads to nonacademic preoccupations outside the classroom, laboratory, or library carrel. However the academician may use it at the outset, unionism, is, in fact, a technique for acquiring authority. Just beyond the faculty's effort to assure intellectual authority over educational policy is the lunge toward a greater voice in budgets and long-range physical planning. In turn, this faculty preoccupation can lead to resistance from the administration, which becomes intent on preserving its own authority. In the process, faculty can lose much of the benign authority they enjoy within the university. Usually they are no match for administrators in the games of power. All the while, performance in the classroom may be deteriorating and less research may be completed.

Only at the University of Connecticut does the contract express an appreciation of the difference between bargaining unit and faculty. In their treatment of governance, the two parties deem it desirable for governance to be shared "so that faculty will have a mechanism and procedure, independent of the collective bargaining process, for making recommendations to appropriate administrative officials and to the Board of Trustees, and for resolving academic matters."[56] There is some sophistication in this formulation.

Most contracts allow for union intercession into the business of the university insofar as information and data on its operations are shared with union representatives in order to facilitate the implementation of the contract. In addition, administrators meet periodically with the union to discuss matters pertaining to the contract's terms. In some cases, such as Western Michigan, the union is permitted to send an observer to meetings of the board of trustees, a right, incidentally, which it probably shares with the general public. In the New Jersey system, the union has the privilege of speaking at all public meetings of the board.

At Bridgeport the union moves a step further. It assumes the faculty's responsibility for participation in program evaluation. Proposals from a union committee, working with the dean of planning, are submitted to regular university committees for review and introduction into the remainder of the governance process. The Western Michigan contract allows the union to nominate faculty representatives to all-university committees. Thus the selection of committee members is by a means in which the university or its divisions have no voice. In the New Jersey system, the union is permitted to appoint one representative to each collegewide committee on which the faculty may already be represented. The possibility thereby arises that in the discussion of any issue faculty and union points of view may differ. As curious as it may seem, the faculty can actually meet itself coming the other way.

In the New Jersey contract, the union must be consulted on reduced load for any member of the bargaining unit and on any changes in policy pertaining to faculty load—matters that would normally concern departments and faculty senates, respectively. The college calendar is also developed in cooperation with the union. The concept involved in union intercession in New Jersey is apparently more the desire to assure equal treatment of all faculty members than to participate in the actual management of the college. Individual faculty can see, therefore, a potential value in the practice.

But the contradictions of such a structure are also apparent. In the Western Michigan contract, the faculty senate is actually enjoined from impinging upon the rights of the bargaining unit. At Bridgeport, the union takes the precaution to assure that neither the university senate nor the faculty council takes action that repeals, rescinds, or modifies the terms and conditions of the collective bargaining agreement. Evidently some union members are not altogether at ease with the idea of collective "faculty" action. Could it be that within this context they fear that on some issue or another the faculty might side with the administration against the union?

Although contracts show the suspicion of the academician toward the institutional aspects of the university, they also reflect a certain distrust of the academician on the part of administrators. Mutual distrust is evident in a number of ways, but none is more pronounced than the attention devoted to personnel files. Contracts specify those materials that may be included, those items that may not be included (anonymous letters or statements relating to the faculty member), and those who may have access to the file. Under many contracts, each time an administrator looks into a file the event must be recorded. Union representatives in most cases may review the file of a bargaining unit member only on written permission from that individual. Moreover, each individual is assured the availability of his personnel file almost on demand. The nature of these provisions makes files a virtual obsession for faculty and perhaps for administrators.

At the University of Connecticut, faculty are allowed to maintain a log that lists and dates all material placed in the file. Both employee and department head sign the log and retain a copy. The Fairleigh Dickinson contract requires that all material in the file carry the college dean's official stamp as well as the date on which the document was received by the dean's office. Pages of the file must be numbered sequentially. Copies of the official file are retained by departments. At Connecticut there is also the right of petition to remove any material that predates the contract. At Northern Iowa, Maine, and in the Pennsylvania system a faculty member may inspect his file only in the presence of an administrator.

An aura of suspicion surrounds the entire business. It reveals a situation in which a legal record rather than relationships among people working within an institutional setting will supposedly determine the outcome of some unspecified future situation. The atmosphere is one of fear that somehow an occasion will arise that will redound adversely upon the employee-employer relationship, almost as if by clever manipulation of a file one or the other side could trick an adversary unfairly. Perhaps the apprehension of faculty is more understandable than the antics of some administrators who negotiate these contract provisions. More than likely, in the consideration of files, administrators use contracts as a device for heightening the institutional as opposed to the collegial profile of the university. Perhaps in some way they see themselves as garnering authority from it.

In reviewing contracts it is always a temptation to speculate from the contents over the relations that exist between faculty and administrators at a particular university. The lengthy (forty thousand words) and explicit contract at Fairleigh Dickinson, for example, suggests a legacy of bad relations or perhaps a faculty that is uncertain about its role. What sort of atmosphere is conveyed when the contract, in specifying causes for dismissal of a faculty member, includes not just gross incompetence or negligence but also willful disregard for scholarly or professional standards, conviction for felony, mental illness, and subverting the rights and welfare of members of the college community? Civility would seem to suggest that these things be left unsaid. The caveat included in the Maine contract to the effect that decisions of the president on some matters are final and not grievable also raises questions. Is the administration uncertain of itself or excessively overbearing? Certainly this wording implies a disregard for collegiality.

Unusual items that are selected for special attention also cast doubts about the relationship between faculty and administration. What real or imagined encroachment prompted one party or the other to inisist on including some obscure matter in the contract? Voluntary attendance at commencement and the process for selecting deans at St. John's, over two hundred words devoted to parking at Fairleigh Dickinson, distinguished faculty awards and the treatment of independent study in the Pennsylvania system, nontraditional assignments at Bridgeport, teaching in outreach centers at Maine, administrative removal of a chairperson in the Minnesota system, and faculty evaluation of administrators or allowances for "nepotism" at Western Michigan all fall into this category. Something surrounding each situation apparently in somebody's view required regulation if the full rights of faculty or administration were to be protected. The significance of such items need not be monumental for them to find their way into a contract. Any of them could have been viewed as a challenge to academic freedom, program integrity, or departmental prerogatives, depending on the circumstances in which they became a subject of contention.

Political Process—Direct Participation and Rationality

In Chapter 5, two points were made about academic politics. They are organized around values. The academician is uncomfortable with the representative function in parliamentary bodies; direct and personal communications are preferred. Finally, in his politics the academician has an abiding belief in rational solution. Collective bargaining agreements demonstrate these principles nicely.

Perhaps the clearest statement of direct and open communication is found in the contract of the University of Cincinnati. In this instance, governance is predicated on the necessity for communication among constituents rather than on achieving a political outcome—the purpose of politics in our open society: "The variety and complexity of tasks performed by institutions of higher education produces an interdependence among the constituent elements of the University. Adequate communication is, therefore, essential and there must be full opportunity for appropriate joint planning and effort."[57] Questions can be raised about the portion of this prescription that suggests undue interdependence among constituent elements of the university. It is a counter to the academician's independence. And institution presupposes a certain amount of interdependence, and as used in this statement, the term may simply suggest a justification for requiring the administration to engage faculty in the operation of the university.

Thereafter, the Cincinnati contract lists twelve illustrations of shared responsibility, most of which assure the right of some unit of the faculty to give "aid, advice, and counsel" to the appropriate administrative office. The contract allows the university's faculty to consider matters affecting the university and gives the faculty sufficient time to counsel the administration, the board of trustees, and the AAUP. Each college's faculty shall advise the dean and each department's faculty its unit head. The faculty's concern is indeed with communication.

Similarly, in the Pennsylvania system, the contract states, "Institutions of higher education are committed to open and rational discussion as a principal means for the clarification of issues and for the solution of problems."[58] The St. John's University contract picks up the same theme in its preamble: "It is further recognized that the roles and responsibilities of the Administration and the faculty are interdependent in the determination and implementation of educational policy and objectives and require the broadest possible cooperation and the fullest exchange of information and opinion with regard to such educational matters."[59] In both cases, it would seem that the purpose of governance can be achieved by open communication even though the political objectives of constituencies may be in conflict. This is a curious academic point of view that would surely mystify a good Boston politician.

In order to allow faculty the opportunity for direct expression, most contracts, including those of Pennsylvania, New Jersey, Maine, Minnesota, and Connecticut, provide for periodic meetings between the president of the university and representatives of the bargaining unit. This practice was noted in our consideration of the academician's treatment of authority. Another observance associated with academic politics that centers on open communication is the right of each individual to speak for himself on all decisions pertaining to personal actions. In the Pennsylvania system, candidates may appear before the promotion and tenure committees to state their cases. Virtually all grievance procedures are also predicated on direct expression by the grievant and open discussion of the purported issue.

Under most contracts (Western Michigan, Fairleigh Dickinson, the University of Northern Iowa, the New Jersey system, and Bridgeport), each individual can respond to anything placed in his personnel file. Only in the presence of all information and all arguments can the academician apparently experience a sense of rationality. Anyone having experience in a bureaucracy knows that this is a poor practice. It is virtually impossible to answer a reprimand or criticism without sounding mean, petty, spiteful, or petulant. After all, the very purpose of a response is to be self-serving. The old pros in institutional politics, therefore, advise against it. But the academician's belief in resolution of differences by direct and rational discourse makes this advice unintelligible. Each individual must have his say, and well-phrased argument will surely convince others of the error of the decision. As a result, much of the injury suffered by faculty in the personnel process is self-inflicted. The futility of a response is often revealed by asking the respondent what he really hopes to achieve by making a statement. Few can think of any reason other than to "set the record straight." This explanation may be sound for the individual seeking personally to uphold values. The focus is on the advocacy of justice. But it is worthless in any sense of institutional purpose—any attempt to influence the actions of an organization.

Out of necessity, the collective voice of the faculty is conveyed in any committee proceedings. Thus, the representative function cannot be avoided altogether in academic politics. Nevertheless, as these examples demonstrate, emphasis in many contracts is on faculty advice as the preferred means of political expression rather than through the act of electing a representative, which is commonly viewed as political expression in the pluralistic system of our country's politics. In the academician's thinking, there is apparently something personal and, therefore, more acceptable about the first of these two ideas.

The compulsion to engage in direct communication derives, of course, from the belief that political process rests on rationality. Contracts demonstrate this proclivity on the part of the academician in two ways. First, there is a preoccupation with information—the substance of rational decisions. Contracts generally are intent upon requiring the administration to share with the bargaining unit all varieties of information about the affairs of the college. Information on the meetings and agenda of board of trustees, the university budget, and rules, regulations, and policies of the college must be made available to the union. The Bridgeport contract has a special article entitled "Information to AAUP." The same concern is found in the contracts of Minnesota, Fairleigh Dickinson, Cincinnati, and others. The one limitation most administrations place on this free flow of information is that they not be required to compile special information requested by the union. The bargaining unit must be content with the information and in the form that it is generated by the university for conducting its business.

The other aspect of rational process reflected in contracts is the necessity for administrators to give reasons for their actions. This, too, was considered in the faculty's view of authority. Just about any candidacy, proposal, or suggestion from faculty that is not accepted by the administration requires a reasonable explanation.

At Cincinnati, where reasons must also be given for all negative personnel decisions, we encounter the zenith of rational politics. New material that becomes available after the personnel selection and promotion process has begun may be added to a candidate's file. In addition, all candidates are guaranteed reconsideration if their application is rejected. The process can be without end. It is apparent that the academician finds only a "rational outcome" acceptable, that is, one that meets his arguments and expectations. At Bridgeport, reconsideration of promotion or tenure decisions is required whenever a candidate adjudges that an error has occurred in procedure or in the application of criteria and weights. Again, the candidate's rational premise is that the information he has presented (the record) justifies the promotion or tenure he desires. Otherwise he would not have applied. After all, he is rational. Any disappointment is bound to have been the result of something going awry. Thus, any negative decision must be reexamined and the error detected. Union contracts reinforce the tendency of faculty to badger deans and presidents over negative decisions, always with seemingly rational arguments for why the outcome should have been different.

The essence of rationality attributed to information is found at the University of Northern Iowa. In this case, a basis for appeal in negative personnel decisions is the faculty member's having had "reasonable expectations based on representations in writing made to him or her by authorized university administrators that the faculty member would be reappointed, granted tenure, or promoted."[60] Such a provision can often be traced to the practice at most universities of giving the overwhelming majority of faculty something above a "satisfactory" rating in personnel evaluations. Departments normally initiate evaluations, and high ratings are shaped by the distaste faculty find in assessing peers. Generally, ratings tell nothing about the quality of performance. They are an expression of approbation due colleagues who uphold collegiality. When confronted with a rejection of an application for promotion, tenure, or reappointment, the individual concerned will immediately point to the "outstanding" or "commendable" performance ratings from peers over the preceding six years and inquire as to the rationality of the rejection in the face of this evidence. The administrator is hard pressed to respond because he probably reviewed and approved the original ratings rather than anger the entire faculty by demanding "honest" evaluations.

More can be said about faculty contracts. This review may be sufficient, however, to show that they reflect the academician's sense of reality—the Cartesian values. A major purpose of faculty in concluding contracts is to stabilize and protect these values in the presence of pressure for change from countervailing forces in our society. The irony of the situation is that to the extent faculties permit their unions to adopt a collective concept of work, they can create a monster of their own that contradicts the tradition of the academic perception. The result can be contrary to the proposition that learning and creativity are inherently linked to the style and symbols of the academic culture.

A great deal of the growth and innovation espoused by society for our colleges and universities, and the concomitant centralization of the administration of public institutions by state governments, ignore the association of creativity with academic style. The challenge for those who would control the academy from beyond its walls and convert the curriculum to a relatively narrow social purpose is to recognize that although such an approach may allow for greater efficiency, it can also mean new political problems and new issues of definition for higher education. As an ever-widening range of forces becomes involved in the university, the academician, for the first time, must concern himself with being politically effective. He is no longer able to rest his claim to preeminence in matters of educational policy on the assertion of the faculty's higher mission. Changes forced upon him necessitate adjustments in his values. Ultimately he can find himself confronting limitations on his intellectual pursuits. At that point, the place of creativity can be questioned. Will it continue to reside in our universities? No academician can, of course, be left totally unfettered by the concerns of our society for higher education. Nevertheless, the greatest loss for higher education may occur on that day when conditions compel the academician to abandon his primary symbol—faculty as university.

Notes

Chapter 1

1. *Chronicle of Higher Education*, July 6, 1981, p. 10; September 16, 1981, p. 8.

2. *Washington Post*, January 28, 1980, p. 1.

3. Leon D. Epstein, *Governing the University* (San Francisco: Jossey-Bass, 1974), p. 18.

4. *Chronicle of Higher Education*, October 10, 1978, p. 15.

5. Ibid., June 15, 1981, p. 10; June 29, 1981, p. 5; July 6, 1981, p. 8; July 27, 1981, pp. 2, 16; August 3, 1981, p. 6; September 16, 1981, p. 8.

6. Ibid., April 16, 1979, p. 3.

7. J. M. Cameron, *On the Idea of a University* (Toronto: University of Toronto Press, 1978), pp. 6, 33, and 36.

8. J. Victor Baldridge et al., *Policy Making and Effective Leadership* (San Francisco: Jossey-Bass, 1978), p. 45.

9. Everett Carll Ladd, Jr., and Seymour Martin Lipset, *Academics, Politics and the 1972 Election*, Domestic Affairs Studies (Washington, D.C.: American Enterprise Institute for Public Policy Research, 1973); Ladd and Lipset, "The Big Differences among Faculty Unions," *Chronicle of Higher Education*, March 13, 1978, p. 14.

Chapter 2

1. American Association of University Professors, Statement of Principles on Academic Freedom and Tenure 1940, cited in William R. Keast, ed., *Faculty Tenure* (San Francisco: Jossey-Bass, 1973), pp. 249−53.

2. Talcott Parsons and Gerald M. Platt, "Considerations on the American Academic System," *Minerva*, 6 (Summer 1968):503.

3. Paul L. Dressel and William H. Faricy, *Return to Responsibility* (San Francisco: Jossey-Bass, 1972), pp. 16−17.

4. Bruce R. Williams, "University Values and University Organization," *Minerva* 10 (April 1972):274.

5. Clark Kerr, *The Uses of the University* (Cambridge: Harvard University Press, 1963), pp. 14−15.

6. Jacques Barzun, *The American University* (New York: Harper and Row, 1968), p. 19.

7. René Descartes, *Discourse on Method and Other Writings*, trans. with introduction by F. E. Sutcliffe (Baltimore: Penguin Books, 1968), pp. 39–52, passim.

8. Ibid., p. 39.

9. Ibid., p. 40.

10. Ibid., p. 43.

11. Ibid., pp. 49–50.

12. Ibid., pp. 39–40.

13. Ibid., pp. 51–52.

14. Robert Paul Wolff, *The Ideal of the University* (Boston: Beacon Press, 1969), pp. 99–101.

15. Bell quoted in Stephen R. Graubard, "Governance in Universities I," in *The Embattled University*, ed. Stephen R. Graubard and Gino A. Ballotti (New York: George Braziller, 1970), p. 254.

16. Herbert A. Simon, *The Sciences of the Artificial* (Cambridge: Massachusetts Institute of Technology Press, 1969), p. 7.

17. Wolff, *The Ideal of the University*, pp. 99–101.

18. Susan Schiefelbein, "Confusion at Harvard," *Saturday Review*, April 1, 1978, pp. 12–22.

19. Baldridge et al., *Policy Making and Effective Leadership*, pp. 107–11.

20. James T. Farrell, "How Studs Lonigan Was Written," in *The League of Frightened Philistines and Other Papers* (New York: Vanguard Press, 1945), p. 81.

21. Parsons and Platt, "Considerations on the American Academic System," p. 521.

22. Baldridge et al., *Policy Making and Effective Leadership*, pp. 107–11.

23. Paul L. Dressel, R. Craig Johnson, and Philip M. Marcus, *The Confidence Crisis* (San Francisco: Jossey-Bass, 1970), pp. 108–9.

24. Descartes, *Discourse on Method and Other Writings*, pp. 39–40.

25. Kerr, *The Uses of the University*, pp. 14–23, passim.

26. Martin Trow, "Reflections on the Transition from Mass to Universal Higher Education," in *The Embattled University*, p. 32.

27. Robert Nisbet, *The Degradation of the Academic Dogma* (New York: Basic Books, 1970), pp. 35, 37.

28. Dressel and Faricy, *Return to Responsibility*, p. 45.

29. F. M. Cornford, *Microcosmographia Academia, Being a Guide for the Young Academic Politician*, 6th ed. (Cambridge, England: Bowes and Bowes, 1964), pp. 5, 12, 17.

Chapter 3

1. Max Weber, *The Theory of Social and Economic Organization*, trans. A. R. Henderson and Talcott Parsons (New York: Free Press, 1968), p. 148.

2. Barzun, *The American University*, p. 4.

3. Dressel, Johnson, and Marcus, *The Confidence Crisis*, p. 48.

4. Clark Kerr, "Governance and Function," in *The Embattled University*, p. 114; Talcott Parsons, *Politics and Social Structure* (New York: Free Press, 1969), pp. 503–7.

5. University of California, *The Culture of the University: Governance and Education*, The Majority Report of the Study Commission on University Governance (San Francisco: Jossey-Bass, 1968), pp. 64–66.

6. *Chronicle of Higher Education*, September 11, 1978, p. 1.

7. Trow, "Reflections on the Transition from Mass to Universal Higher Education," p. 31.

8. Dean E. McHenry and Associates, *Academic Departments* (San Francisco: Jossey-Bass, 1977), Chapters 5, 6, 7, and 8.

9. *Humanities* 4, nos. 2–3 (April–June 1974):2.

10. Barzun, *The American University*, p. 18.

11. University of California, *The Culture of the University*, pp. 64–66.

12. Sidney Verba, *Small Groups and Political Behavior* (Princeton: Princeton University Press, 1961), pp. 27–29, 40.

13. Barry E. Collins and Harold Guetzkow, *A Social Psychology of Group Process for Decision Making* (New York: John Wiley and Sons, 1964), pp. 54–55.

14. John W. Thibaut and Harold H. Kelley, *The Social Psychology of Groups* (New York: John Wiley and Sons, 1969), pp. 263, 272.

15. David Riesman, *Constraint and Variety in American Education* (Lincoln: University of Nebraska Press, 1958), p. 24.

16. John Dewey, *Democracy and Education* (New York: Free Press, 1966), pp. 335–36.

17. Herbert A. Simon, *Models of Man* (New York: John Wiley and Sons, 1957), p. 122.

18. Riesman, *Constraint and Variety in American Education*, pp. 58, 66–67.

19. Dressel, Johnson, and Marcus, *The Confidence Crisis*, p. 78.

20. Verba, *Small Groups and Political Behavior*, p. 27.

Chapter 4

1. Eric Ashby, *Adapting Universities to Technological Society* (San Francisco: Jossey-Bass, 1974), pp. 98–100; Baldridge et al., *Policy Making and Effective Leadership*, pp. 71, 74; Epstein, *Governing the University*, p. 107; Kenneth P. Mortimer and T. R. McConnell, *Sharing Authority Effectively* (San Francisco: Jossey-Bass, 1978), pp. 269–74.

2. Mortimer and McConnell, *Sharing Authority Effectively*, p. 6.

3. University of California, *The Culture of the University*, p. 65.

4. Connecticut State College Faculty Federation (CSFT-AFT, AFL-CIO) *A Statement to College Teaching Faculty* (West Hartford: Connecticut State Federation of Teachers, undated).

5. *Chronicle of Higher Education*, February 26, 1979, p. 9.

6. Ibid., October 2, 1978, p. 14.

7. Ibid., June 26, 1978, p. 3.

8. Mancur Olson, Jr., *The Logic of Collective Action* (Cambridge: Harvard University Press, 1965), pp. 21, 28–29, 46.

9. *Chronicle of Higher Education*, August 25, 1980, p. 11; September 16, 1981, p. 8.

10. Weber, *The Theory of Social and Economic Organization*, pp. 412–13.

11. Ibid., pp. 398–99, 415.

12. Dressel, Johnson, and Marcus, *The Confidence Crisis*, p. 11.

13. University of California, *The Culture of the University*, pp. 61–62.

14. Barzun, *The American University*, pp. 34–40.

15. Herbert Simon, *Administrative Behavior* (New York: Macmillan, 1961), p. 13.

16. Alvin W. Gouldner, "Cosmopolitans and Locals: Toward an Analysis of Latent Roles—I," *Administrative Science Quarterly* 2 (June 1957):285–86.

17. These and preceding job titles were taken from the Placement Section of the *Chronicle of Higher Education*.

18. "John Silber after '60 Minutes,'" *Educational Review*, Spring 1980, pp. 18–24.

Chapter 5

1. Robert Paul Wolff, *The Poverty of Liberalism* (Boston: Beacon Press, 1968), pp. 192–94.

2. Michael Oakeshott, *Rationalism in Politics* (London: Methuen, 1962), pp. 1–2.

3. David Braybooke and Charles E. Lindbloom, *A Strategy of Decision* (Glencoe: Free Press, 1963), pp. 9–11.

4. Ibid., p. 14.

5. Dressel, Johnson, and Marcus, *The Confidence Crisis*, p. 55.

6. David Riesman, *On Higher Education*, Prepared for the Carnegie Council on Policy Studies in Higher Education (San Francisco: Jossey-Bass, 1980), p. 274; Gerald Grant and David Riesman, *The Perpetual Dream: Reform and Experiment in the American College* (Chicago: University of Chicago Press, 1978), pp. 325–46; Harold L. Hodgkinson, *Campus Senate Experiment in Democracy* (Berkeley: University of California Press, 1974), p. 46.

7. Weber, *The Theory of Social and Economic Organization*, p. 417.

8. Edmund Burke, "Speech at the Conclusion of the Poll in Bristol, November 3, 1774," in *Edmund Burke on Revolution*, ed. Robert A. Smith (New York: Harper and Row, 1968), pp. 52–54.

9. Robert A. Dahl, *A Preface to Democratic Theory* (Chicago: Univeristy of Chicago Press, Phoenix Books, 1956), pp. 4, 10–16.

10. Theodore J. Lowi, *The End of Liberalism* (New York: Norton, 1969), pp. 9–12, 44–49.

11. William E. Connolly, "The Challenge of Pluralistic Theory," in *The*

Basis of Pluralism, ed. William E. Connolly (New York: Atherton Press, 1969), pp. 4, 9–12, 18.

12. University of California, *The Culture of the University,* pp. 18, 22, 25–33.

13. Oakeshott, *Rationalism in Politics,* p. 5.

14. Edmund Burke, *Reflections on the Revolution in France,* ed. Conor Cruise O'Brien (Baltimore: Penguin Books, 1968), pp. 101, 105, 115–19, 135, 193, and 261; Burke, "Speech at the Conclusion of the Poll in Bristol," p. 53; "An Appeal from the New to the Old Whigs, 1791," in *Edmund Burke on Revolution,* p. 168.

15. Cornford, *Microcosmographia Academia,* pp. 25–26.

16. Judith N. Shklar, "Decisionism," in *Rational Decision,* NOMOS VII, ed. Carl J. Friedrich, (New York: Atherton Press, 1964), pp. 7, 9.

17. Kerr, *The Uses of the University,* p. 36.

18. Lewis B. Mayhew, "Faculty in Campus Governance," in *Agony and Promise,* ed. G. Kerry Smith (San Francisco: Jossey-Bass, 1969), p. 156; Howard R. Bowen, "Governance and Educational Reform," in *Agony and Promise,* p. 181.

19. Morris Keeton, "The Disenfranchised on Campus," in *The Troubled Campus,* ed. G. Kerry Smith (San Francisco: Jossey-Bass, 1970), p. 119; Kerr, "Governance and Function," in *The Embattled University,* p. 120; Bowen, "Governance and Educational Reform," in *Agony and Promise,* pp. 181–82.

20. Burke, *Reflections on the Revolution in France,* p. 135.

21. University of California, *The Culture of the University,* pp. 55, 57–64.

22. Michael D. Cohen and James G. March, *Leadership and Ambiguity: The American College President,* A General Report prepared for the Carnegie Commission on Higher Education (New York: McGraw-Hill Book Company, 1974), pp. 30–36, 196–97, 206–8, 212.

23. Ladd and Lipset, *Academics, Politics and the 1972 Election,* pp. 6, 8, 16.

24. Ibid., pp. 18–21.

Chapter 6

1. *Chronicle of Higher Education,* July 26, 1978, p. 8; July 7, 1980, p. 7; July 27, 1981, p. 2.

2. Everett Carll Ladd, Jr., and Seymour Martin Lipset, "Faculty Support for Unionization," *Chronicle of Higher Education,* February 13, 1978, p. 8; Ladd and Lipset, "The Big Differences among Faculty Unions," p. 14.

3. *Agreement, The State of New Jersey, Council of New Jersey State College Locals NJSFT-AFT, AFL-CIO, State College Units,* July 1, 1977–June 30, 1979, Preamble, p. 1.

4. *Collective Bargaining Agreement between Association of Pennsylvania State College and University Faculties and Commonwealth of Pennsylvania,* Effective September 1, 1974, p. 1.

5. *Collective Bargaining Agreement by and between University of*

Bridgeport and University of Bridgeport Chapter, American Association of University Professors, September 1, 1978, Preamble, p. 1.

6. *Agreement between University of Cincinnati and AAUP, University of Cincinnati Chapter,* September 1, 1979 to August 31, 1981, Preamble.

7. *Agreement between Western Michigan University and the WMU AAUP Chapter,* October 24, 1978—September 1, 1981, p. 1.

8. *University of Maine Agreement with Associated Faculties of the University of Maine Faculty Unit,* July 1979 to June 1981, Article 2, p. 3, and Article 3, p. 4.

9. *Agreement between Fairleigh Dickinson University and Fairleigh Dickinson University Council of American Association of University Professors Chapters,* September 1, 1974—August 31, 1976, Preamble.

10. *Agreement between the Administration of St. John's University, New York and the St. John's Chapter of the American Associaton of University Professors—Faculty Associaton at St. John's University,* 1974—1977, Preamble, p. 1.

11. *University of Cincinnati/AAUP,* Article 2, p. 2.

12. *Association of Faculties/Commonwealth of Pennsylvania,* Article 2, p. 3.

13. *University of Cincinnati/AAUP,* Article 7, p. 17.

14. *Western Michigan University/AAUP,* Appendix A, p. 71.

15. *Agreement between State University Board for the State of Minnesota and Inter-Faculty Organization/Minnesota Education Association,* Effective through June 30, 1977, Article 25, pp. 26—27.

16. *St. John's University/AAUP,* Article 27, p. 31.

17. *Association of Faculties/Commonwealth of Pennsylvania,* Article 19, p. 25.

18. *University of Bridgeport/AAUP,* Article 8, p. 32.

19. Ibid., Article 12, p. 48.

20. Ibid., Article 8, p. 15.

21. *University of Cincinnati/AAUP,* Article 7, p. 16.

22. *Western Michigan University/AAUP,* Article 28, p. 55.

23. *Fairleigh Dickinson University/AAUP,* Article 7, p. 25.

24. *University of Cincinnati/AAUP,* Article 7, p. 17.

25. *University of Maine/Associated Faculties,* Article 23, p. 38.

26. *Fairleigh Dickinson University/AAUP,* Article 7, p. 25.

27. *Collective Bargaining Agreement between the University of Connecticut Board of Trustees and the University of Connecticut Chapter of the American Association of University Professors,* July 1, 1979—June 30, 1981.

28. *A Master Agreement between the State of Iowa Board of Regents and the UNI-United Faculty (AAUP/IHEA),* 1 July 1977—June 1979.

29. *University of Maine/Associated Faculties,* Article 23, p. 38.

30. *Fairleigh Dickinson University/AAUP,* Article 7, p. 32.

31. Ibid., Article 18, p. 132.

32. *University of Cincinnati/AAUP,* Article 29, p. 45.

33. *Western Michigan University/AAUP,* Article 22, p. 37.

34. *University of Bridgeport/AAUP,* Article 8, p. 16.

35. *St. John's University/AAUP,* Article 2, p. 3.

36. *University of Bridgeport, AAUP,* Article 8, p. 22.

37. *State of New Jersey/NJSFT-AFT,* Article 13, p. 19.

38. *St. John's University/AAUP,* Article 5, p. 6.

39. *Fairleigh Dickinson University/AAUP,* Article 10, p. 71.

40. *University of Maine/Associated Faculties,* Article 12, p. 19.

41. *University of Bridgeport/AAUP,* Article 8, p. 19.

42. *Fairleigh Dickinson University/AAUP,* Article 8, p. 36.

43. *St. John's University/AAUP,* Article 9, p. 12.

44. *University of Maine/Associated Faculties,* Article 12, p. 18.

45. Ibid., Article 12, p. 18.

46. *State University Board for the State of Minnesota/Inter-Faculty Organization,* Article 20, p. 18.

47. *Western Michigan University/AAUP,* Article 16, p. 24.

48. *Fairleigh Dickinson University/AAUP,* Article 10, p. 77.

49. *University of Cincinnati/AAUP,* Article 29, p. 44.

50. *Association of Faculties/Commonwealth of Pennsylvania,* Article 27, p. 40.

51. *State of New Jersey/NJSFT-AFT,* Article 13, p. 19.

52. *Western Michigan University/AAUP,* Article 20, p. 37.

53. *State of New Jersey/NJSFT-AFT,* Article 18, p. 62.

54. *Western Michigan University/AAUP,* Article 20, p. 32.

55. *Chronicle of Higher Education,* March 3, 1980, p. 8.

56. *University of Connecticut/AAUP,* Article 4, p. 7.

57. *University of Cincinnati/AAUP,* Article 27, p. 38.

58. *Association of Faculties/Commonwealth of Pennsylvania,* Article 4, p. 4.

59. *St. John's University/AAUP,* Preamble, p. 1.

60. *State of Iowa Board of Regents/AAUP-IHEA,* Article 11, p. 31.

Bibliography

Books

Ashby, Eric. *Adapting Universities to Technological Society.* San Francisco: Jossey-Bass, 1974.

Barzun, Jacques. *The American University.* New York: Harper and Row, 1968.

Baldridge, J. Victor; Curtis, David V.; Ecker, George; and Riley, Gary L. *Policy Making and Effective Leadership.* San Francisco: Jossey-Bass, 1978.

Braybooke, David, and Lindbloom, Charles E. *A Strategy of Decision.* Glencoe: Free Press, 1963.

Burke, Edmund. *Reflections on the Revolution in France.* Edited by Conor Cruise O'Brien. Baltimore: Penguin Books, 1968.

————. "Speech at the Conclusion of the Poll in Bristol, November 3, 1774." In *Edmund Burke on Revolution.* Edited by Robert A. Smith. New York: Harper and Row, 1968.

Cameron, J. M. *On the Idea of a University.* Toronto: University of Toronto Press, 1978.

Cohen, Michael D., and March, James G. *Leadership and Ambiguity: The American College President.* A General Report Prepared for the Carnegie Commission on Higher Education. New York: McGraw-Hill Book Company, 1974.

Collins, Barry E., and Guetzkow, Harold. *A Social Psychology of Group Process for Decision Making.* New York: John Wiley and Sons, 1964.

Cornford, F. M. *Microcosmographia, Being a Guide for the Young Academic Politician.* 6th ed. Cambridge, England: Bowes and Bowes, 1964.

Dahl, Robert A. *A Preface to Democratic Theory.* Chicago: University of Chicago Press, Phoenix Books, 1956.

Descartes, René. *Discourse on Method and Other Writings.* Translated with an Introduction by F. E. Sutcliffe. Baltimore: Penguin Books, 1968.

Dewey, John. *Democracy and Education.* New York: Free Press, 1966.

Dressel, Paul L., and Faricy, William H. *Return to Responsibility.* San Francisco: Jossey-Bass, 1972.

Dressel, Paul L.; Johnson, F. Craig; and Marcus, Philip M. *The Confidence Crisis.* San Francisco: Jossey-Bass, 1970.

Epstein, Leon D. *Governing the University.* San Francisco: Jossey-Bass, 1974.

Grant, Gerald, and Riesman, David. *The Perpetual Dream: Reform and Experiment in the American College.* Chicago: University of Chicago Press, 1978.

Hodgkinson, Harold L. *Campus Senate Experiment in Democracy.* Berkeley: University of California Press, 1974.

Kerr, Clark. *The Uses of the University.* Cambridge: Harvard University Press, 1963.

Ladd, Everett Carll, Jr., and Lipset, Seymour Martin. *Academics, Politics and the 1972 Election.* Domestic Affairs Series. Washington, D.C.: American Enterprise Institute for Public Policy Research, 1973.

Lowi, Theodore J. *The End of Liberalism.* New York: Norton, 1969.

McHenry, Dean E., and Associates. *Academic Departments.* San Francisco: Jossey-Bass, 1977.

Mortimer, Kenneth P., and McConnell, T. R. *Sharing Authority Effectively.* San Francisco: Jossey-Bass, 1978.

Nisbet, Robert. *The Degradation of the Academic Dogma.* New York: Basic Books, 1970.

Oakeshott, Michael. *Rationalism in Politics.* London: Methuen, 1962.

Olson, Mancur, Jr. *The Logic of Collective Action.* Cambridge: Harvard University Press, 1965.

Parsons, Talcott. *Politics and Social Structure.* New York: Free Press, 1969.

Riesman, David. *Constraint and Variety in American Education.* Lincoln: University of Nebraska Press, 1958.

————. *On Higher Education.* Prepared for the Carnegie Council on Policy Studies in Higher Education. San Francisco: Jossey-Bass, 1980.

Simon, Herbert A. *Administrative Behavior.* New York: Macmillan, 1961.

————. *Models of Man.* New York: John Wiley and Sons, 1957.

————. *The Sciences of the Artificial.* Cambridge: Massachusetts Institute of Technology Press, 1969.

Thibaut, John W., and Kelley, Harold H. *The Social Psychology of Groups.* New York: John Wiley and Sons, 1969.

University of California. *The Culture of the University: Governance and Education.* The Majority Report of the Study Commission on University Governance. San Francisco: Jossey-Bass, 1968.

Verba, Sidney. *Small Groups and Political Behavior.* Princeton: Princeton University Press, 1961.

Weber, Max. *The Theory of Social and Economic Organization.* Translated by A. R. Henderson and Talcott Parsons. Edited with an Introduction by Talcott Parsons. New York: Free Press, 1968.

Wolff, Robert Paul. *The Ideal of the University.* Boston: Beacon Press, 1969.

————. *The Poverty of Liberalism.* Boston: Beacon Press, 1968.

Articles in Edited Works

Bowen, Howard R. "Governance and Educational Reform." In *Agony and*

Promise, edited by G. Kerry Smith. San Francisco: Jossey-Bass, 1969.

Connolly, William E. "The Challenge of Pluralistic Theory." In *The Bias of Pluralism,* edited by William E. Connolly. New York: Atherton Press, 1969.

Farrell, James T. "How Studs Lonigan Was Written." In *The League of Frightened Philistines and Other Papers,* edited by James T. Farrell. New York: Vanguard Press, 1945.

Graubard, Stephen R. "Governance in Universities I." In *The Embattled University,* edited by Stephen R. Graubard and Gino A. Ballotti. New York: George Braziller, 1970.

Keeton, Morris. "The Disenfranchised on Campus." In *The Troubled Campus,* edited by G. Kerry Smith. San Francisco: Jossey-Bass, 1970.

Kerr, Clark. "Governance and Function." In *The Embattled University,* edited by Stephen R. Graubard and Gino A. Ballotti. New York: George Braziller, 1970.

Mayhew, Lewis B. "Faculty in Campus Governance." In *Agony and Promise,* edited by G. Kerry Smith. San Francisco: Jossey-Bass, 1969.

Shklar, Judith N. "Decisionism." In *Rational Decision,* NOMOS VII, edited by Carl J. Friedrich. New York: Atherton Press, 1964.

Trow, Martin. "Reflections on the Transition from Mass to Universal Higher Education." In *The Embattled University,* edited by Stephen R. Graubard and Gino A. Ballotti. New York: George Braziller, 1970.

Articles in Journals and Periodicals

Gouldner, Alvin W. "Cosmopolitans and Locals: Toward an Analysis of Latent Roles—I." *Administrative Science Quarterly* 2 (June 1957): 281−306.

"John Silber after '60 Minutes.'" *Educational Review,* Spring 1980, pp. 18−24.

Ladd, Everett Carll, Jr., and Lipset, Seymour Martin. "The Big Differences among Faculty Unions." *Chronicle of Higher Education,* March 13, 1978, p. 14.

————. "Faculty Support for Unionization." *Chronicle of Higher Education,* February 13, 1978, p. 8.

Parsons, Talcott, and Platt, Gerald M. "Considerations on the American Academic System." *Minerva* 6 (Summer 1968):497−523.

Schiefelbein, Susan. "Confusion at Harvard." *Saturday Review,* April 1, 1978, pp. 12−22.

Williams, Bruce R. "University Values and University Organization." *Minerva* 10 (April 1972):259−79.

Documents

Agreement between the Administration of St. John's University, New York and the St. John's Chapter of the American Association of University

Professors—Faculty Association at St. John's University, 1974—1977.

Agreement between Fairleigh Dickinson University and Fairleigh Dickinson University Council of American Association of University Professors Chapters, September 1, 1974—August 31, 1976.

Agreement between State University Board for the State of Minnesota and Inter-Faculty Organization/Minnesota Education Association, Effective through June 30, 1977.

Agreement between University of Cincinnati and AAUP, University of Cincinnati Chapter, September 1, 1979 to August 31, 1981.

Agreement between Western Michigan University and the WMU AAUP Chapter, October 24, 1978—September 1, 1981.

Agreement, The State of New Jersey, Council of New Jersey State College Locals NJSFT-AFT, AFL-CIO, State College Units, July 1, 1977—June 30, 1979.

American Association of University Professors. Statement of Principles on Academic Freedom and Tenure 1940. In *Faculty Tenure,* edited by William R. Keast. San Francisco: Jossey-Bass, 1973.

Collective Bargaining Agreement between Association of Pennsylvania State College and University Faculties and Commonwealth of Pennsylvania, Effective September 1, 1974.

Collective Bargaining Agreement between the University of Connecticut Board of Trustees and the University of Connecticut Chapter of the American Association of University Professors, July 1, 1979—June 30, 1981.

Collective Bargaining Agreement by and between University of Bridgeport and University of Bridgeport Chapter, American Association of University Professors, September 1, 1978.

Connecticut State College Faculty Federation (CSFT-AFT, AFL-CIO). *A Statement to State College Teaching Faculty.* West Hartford: Connecticut State Federation of Teachers, undated.

A Master Agreement between the State of Iowa Board of Regents and the UNI-United Faculty (AAUP/IHEA), July 1977—June 1979.

University of Maine Agreement with Associated Faculties of the University of Maine Faculty Unit, July 1979 to June 1981.

Newspapers and Periodicals

Chronicle of Higher Education
Humanities
New York Times
Washington Post

Index

Academic freedom, 17, 130, 132

Academicians: liberalism of, 5; working practices, 10, 27, 53; and independence, 10, 129, 132; view of institution, 22, 35, 166; concept of power, 22, 51, 61–62, 79–86, 111, 122; as evaluator of peers, 25; concept of balance, 29–34; view of resource allocation, 31–32; use of authority, 62; concept of institutional growth, 28–29; concept of time, 33–34, 50, 65, 129, 141–45; concept of responsibility, 38–39, 61, 138–39; loyalties, 45, 55; and self-interest, 46, 51, 55–58; concept of security, 51, 100; and choice, 55; and acquisitiveness, 56, 57; concept of emotion and intellect, 57; and social reality, 58; interaction with administrators, 68, 167; view of collegiality, 71; and bureaucratic process, 72; and decision making, 73; view of educational policy, 79; concept of professional environment, 82; local and cosmopolitan attitudes, 89; and approbation, 99–101; as rationalists, 103, 104, 129, 168–69, 171; and harmony, 105; views on governance, 107; concept of progress, 112; and pluralistic politics, 112, 113; dissatisfaction with politics, 115; as moral decisionist, 118; and primacy of individual, 133–35, 137–38, 146; and community service, 139; and outside employment, 144; dual identity under collective bargaining, 75, 165; political effectiveness, 172; style of performance. *See* Style, academic

Administrators, 38, 44–45, 52, 66, 79, 87; concern for education, 68, 69; and academic leadership, 80; power and influence of, 83; view of quasi-administration, 90; organization of, 90–93; style, 93–101; as middle management, 92; personal aspects of performance, 99; and sabbatical leaves, 135; powers of vice-president, 156; responsibilities of, 160–61, 167; required to explain actions, 162–63

Alma mater, 1

Alverno College, 77–78

American Association of University Professors, 128, 129, 170; Statement of Principles on Academic Freedom and Tenure, 132; Professional Code of Ethics, 134

American Federation of Teachers, 74, 128, 129

Antiauthoritarian organization, 86

Antipathies, 65

Appointments: to faculty, 41, 136, 152, 154–55; under collective bargain, 157–58

Arjuna, x

Autonomy, 17, 21, 28

Baldridge, J. Victor, 12, 30–31

Barzun, Jacques, 18, 41, 88

Bell, Daniel, 21, 47

Boston University, 75, 95

Bowen, Howard R., 120–21, 125

Braybooke, David, 102–03, 124

Bridgeport, University of, 75, 131, 136, 137, 142, 144, 146, 154, 156–58, 165, 166, 169, 170, 171

Bureaucracy, 9, 10, 72–76; in universities, 91; growth of, 91–92

Burke, Edmund, 109, 114−15

California, University of: 1967 Majority Report of the Study Commission on University Governance, 44, 51, 71, 88, 111, 122, 125
Cameron, J. M., 6−7
Careerism, 36
Carnegie Survey: 1969, 125−26
Cartesian principles, 18, 19, 21, 24, 25, 33, 37, 39, 47, 50, 52, 63, 65, 85, 89, 92, 95, 96, 111−13, 115, 118, 122, 129, 134, 139, 161, 164, 172
Central Connecticut State College, xi, 78
Chairmen, department, 27, 59, 61, 87, 156−59; election of, 62; excluded from collegium, 158; recall of, 159; removal of, 168
Change, 2, 32, 47, 172
Chenango Valley, 81
Cincinnati, University of, 128, 131−33, 139, 141, 142, 146, 147−49, 153, 155, 157, 158, 160, 168, 170, 171
Classroom visitations, 24, 150−51
Cohen, Michael D., 123−24
Colgate University, xi, 78, 107−08
Colleagueship, 64
Collective bargaining, 56, 74, 75, 100, 127−72; dual identities of faculty under, 75; union in faculty role, 165
Colleges, 30, 31; four-year teaching, 12, 13, 15; university colleges, 44; experimental, 46; state systems, 3, 66; private, 4, 66, 67; boards of trustees, 5, 67, 147; and collective bargaining, 127−72
Collegiality, 40−45, 54, 58, 68, 71, 106, 122, 129, 136, 149−56, 164; organization of, 151−52; authority, 153−55; membership, 41, 154
Columbia University, 70
Commencement: required attendance, 167
Committees, 26, 43, 51, 60, 152, 155, 162, 165, 170
Communication: in academic organization, 41−44, 49, 69, 168−70; vertical, 43−44
Community, 102, 156, 167; rational concept of, 102, 104; direct participation in, 103; and dialogue, 104; service to, 140
Comparison. *See* Competition and comparison
Competition and comparison, 23−29
Connecticut: State College System, 74;

University of, 128, 137, 142, 146, 154, 157, 165, 169
Connolly, William E., 110
Consensus, 63−64
Cornford, F. M., 39, 117−18
Creativity, 14, 15, 28; description of, 12
Criteria syndrome, 153
Curriculum, 35, 37, 43, 46, 56, 57, 153, 162; requirements, 35; program structure, 36, 76−79; honors programs, 45, 76, 78; preceptorials, 45; residence learning, 45; interdisciplinary, 45, 48−49, 54; non-disciplinary, 58; competency-based programs, 77; faculty program responsibilities, 131; independent study, 168

Dahl, Robert, 110
Deans, 142, 151; as middle management, 92; and chairmen, 92; as "faculty man," 94; as Arab rug merchants, 99; disputes with faculty, 155; and faculty appointments, 157; selection of, 167. *See also* Administrators
Decision-making, 51, 150; rational decisions, 105
Departments, 42, 43, 45, 46, 49, 50, 51, 55, 59, 78, 123, 133, 150, 162, 171
Descartes, 18, 19, 21, 36−37, 103, 146. *See also* Cartesian principles
Dewey, John, 57
Disciplines, 42, 45, 46, 49, 50, 57, 133, 149; applied, 14, 36−37
Division of labor, 11, 92
Djakarta, ix
Dressel, Paul, 32, 41, 58−59, 87, 107−08

Enrichment, academic, 28, 32
Entrepreneurial spirit, 6, 39
Esteem, 24, 80, 85
Evaluation, 23−26, 172; by students of courses, 23, 154; questionnaire, 24
Evergreen College, 46

Faculty: as university, 14, 97; commitment, 40
Failure: academicians concept of, 15, 28
Fairleigh Dickinson University, 128, 131−70 passim
Farrell, James T., 28
Featherbedding, 143
Financial exigency, 133

General education, 35, 42, 48, 50, 76
General studies. *See* General education
Giving reasons, 161–63, 170
Goddess of South Seas, x
Gouldner, Alvin, 89
Governance, 68, 75, 108, 119–23, 163; Statement on Government of Colleges and Universities, 69; shared governance, 72, 168; academicians' suspicions of, 107; relation to collective bargain, 75, 164–65
Group goals, 51, 52–55, 111, 130

Hampshire College, 46
Harvard University, 23; School of Public Health, 44
Higher education: humanistic, 2, 3; experiential programs in, 2; efficiency in, 3, 4, 8, 15; state support for, 3, 4; controls over and interference in, 3, 6; institutional income, 3; federal support for, 3, 4, 5; private sector, 4; and national defense, 6; organization of, 41
Hofstadter, Richard, 124

Industry: characteristics of, 10
Innovation. *See* Change
Integration: academic concepts of, 40
Intellectual expression, 9, 33, 38
Interdependence, 21

Javanese reality, x
Jefferson, Thomas, x

Keeton, Morris, 121
Kelley, Harold H., 54, 116
Kerr, Clark, 17, 35, 43, 119–21, 124–25
Kiwanis, 140

Ladd, Everett C., Jr., and Lipset, Seymour Martin, 14, 124–25, 129
Leadership, 61, 111
Legal theorists, 118
Legitimacy, 57, 140
Lindbloom, Charles E., 102–03, 124
Lions Club, 140
Lipset, Seymour Martin. *See* Ladd, Everett C., Jr.
Lowi, Theodore, 110

Madison, James, 110
Maine, University of, 128, 131, 136, 137, 139, 141–44, 146, 154, 157, 162, 167, 169

Management, 6, 7, 8, 15, 56, 66; of department, 152
March, James G., 123–24
Mayhew, Lewis B., 120
Methodology, 47
Miami, University of, 4
Minnesota, State Universities of, 128, 135, 139, 144, 146, 158, 168, 169, 170
Moral decisionist: academician as, 118
Mowgli, x
Multiversity. *See* University

National Education Association, 128, 129
National Endowment for the Arts and Humanities. *See* Higher education, federal support for
National Science Foundation. *See* Higher education, federal support for
Negligence, 145
Nepotism, 168
New Jersey State Colleges, 128, 130, 133, 142, 143, 146, 150, 153, 154, 157, 161, 162, 165, 166, 169
Newman, John Henry, 1
New programs, 32. *See also* Change
Nisbet, Robert, 37
Northern Iowa, University of, 128, 142, 146, 154, 167, 169, 171

Oakeshott, Michael, 102–03, 112–13, 124
Office location, 137
Olson, Mancur, 80
Organization: autocephalous, 41; academic, 43

Parking: as faculty privilege, 168
Parsons, Talcott, 30, 43
Pennsylvania State Colleges and Universities, 128, 130, 132, 136, 142, 146, 150, 151, 154, 157, 161, 167, 168, 169
Personnel files, 136, 151, 166–67
Pine Barrens, 81
Platt, Gerald M., 30
Policy, educational, 34–37, 88, 98, 172
Politics, xi; definition of, 7; academicians' idea of balance in, 29–34; rationalistic, 103–06, 112, 168, 171; pluralistic, 106–11; representative function in, 109, 168–70; public interest in, 110
Power, 111, 122; in business and government, 60; as academic prestige, 80. *See also* Academicians

President: powers of under collective bargain, 157, 161
Pretensions, 15
Princeton University, 4
Professing, 56
Proliferation. *See* Enrichment, academic
Promotion, 30, 42, 100, 136, 152, 162

Quasi-administration, 71, 86–90, 108

Rank, 58–59
Recruitment, 41, 46
Research, 31, 129; organization of, 53–54; funding by government, 85
Resource allocation. *See* Academicians
Retrenchment, 146, 161; procedure at University of Cincinnati, 147–49
Reward structure, 13, 23, 41
Riesman, David, 55, 58, 108
Robert's Rules of Order, 116

Sabbatical leaves, 13, 135–36, 152, 162
St. John's University, 128, 131, 136, 142, 143, 146, 153, 155, 156, 157, 167, 169
St. Mary's College of Maryland, 46
Sanctions and punishment: in academic organization, 62–64, 169–70
Santa Cruz College, 46
Scarcity: academic concept of, 5, 32–33
Self-interest, 15, 55–58
Self-oriented behavior, 51, 54–55, 116
Service: Academician's concept of, 139–40; and outside employment, 144
Shils, Edward, 6
Shklar, Judith, 118–19
Silber, John, 75, 95
Simon, Herbert, 22, 88
Small group theory, 51–64 passim, 87
Society, pluralistic, 47, 103; relation to academic constituencies, 83; concepts of, 106–11; representation in, 106, 115, 170; interest groups, 111
Soviet Union, 84

Stability in working environment, 19, 145–49; and security, 146
Stanford University, 4
State Department, ix
Stockton State College, xi, 47–49, 108–09
Style, academic, 1, 10–11, 53, 111, 122, 153, 172; segmented, 20; pedagogical, 24; entrepreneurial nature of, 119
Sukarno, ix, x
Symbols, 21, 114, 130, 151, 161, 172; faculty as university, 97, 161, 172; academic mission, 146, 150, 172

Teaching load, 13, 33, 141; overload, 142–43; student-faculty ratio, 147
Tenure, 30, 39, 42, 100, 135, 136, 152, 162; terminating tenured faculty, 147
Terminal degree, 11, 39, 132, 150
Thibaut, John W., 54, 116
Tocqueville, Alexis de, 124–25
Trow, Martin, 35, 45

Unions, faculty. *See* Collective bargaining
University: definition of, 1; constituencies, 2, 38, 65, 67; multiversities, 30; antipathies in community, 65; influence of government on, 85; as a business, 95; autonomous and social mission of, 96; nondirective concepts of administration in, 97. *See also* Colleges

Verba, Sidney, 51–52
Vice-president. *See* Administrators

Weber, Max, 41, 86–87, 109
Western Michigan University, 128, 131, 134, 135, 139, 143, 146, 149–54, 157, 161, 162, 163, 165, 166, 168, 169
Wisconsin system, 148
Wolff, Robert, 21, 23, 34, 102–03, 115, 124

Yeshiva University, 164